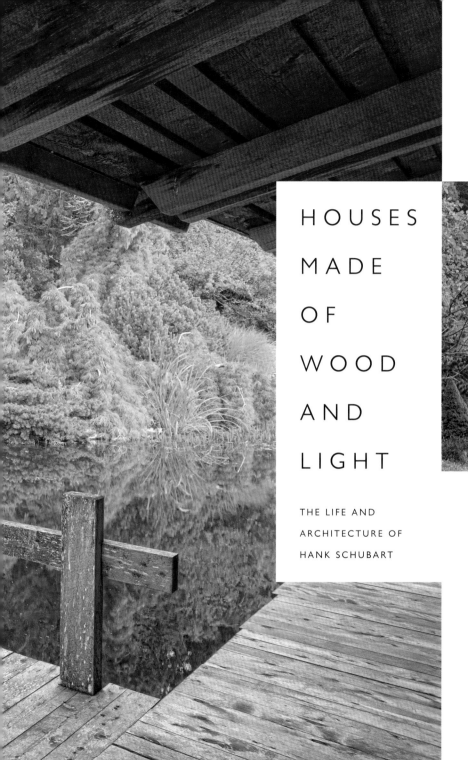

HOUSES MADE OF WOOD AND LIGHT

THE LIFE AND
ARCHITECTURE OF
HANK SCHUBART

BY MICHELE DUNKERLEY

WITH JANE HICKIE

PHOTOGRAPHS BY JIM ALINDER

UNIVERSITY OF TEXAS PRESS, AUSTIN

Publication of this book was made possible in part by support from Roger Fullington and a challenge grant from the National Endowment for the Humanities.

Requests for permission to reproduce material
from this work should be sent to:
Permissions
University of Texas Press
P.O. Box 7819
Austin, TX 78713-7819
www.utexas.edu/utpress/about/bpermission.html

The paper used in this book meets the minimum requirements
of ANSI/NISO Z39.48-1992 (R1997) (Permanence of Paper). ∞

Designed by Lindsay Starr

LIBRARY OF CONGRESS CATALOGING-IN-PUBLICATION DATA

Dunkerley, Michele, 1958–
    Houses made of wood and light : the life and architecture of Hank Schubart /
by Michele Dunkerley with Jane Hickie ; photos by Jim Alinder. — 1st ed.
        p.   cm. — (Roger Fullington series in architecture)
    Includes bibliographical references.
    ISBN 978-0-292-72942-1 (cloth : alk. paper) — ISBN 978-0-292-73714-3 (e-book)
    1. Schubart, Hank, 1916–1998. 2. Architects—United States—Biography.
3. Architecture, Domestic—British Columbia—Saltspring Island—History—
20th century. I. Schubart, Hank, 1916–1998. II. Hickie, Jane. III. Alinder, James.
IV. Title. V. Title: Life and architecture of Hank Schubart.
    NA737.S3555D86 2012
    720.92—dc23   [B]   2011038592

For Jane, for helping me find my way to
Salt Spring Island and other open horizons

CONTENTS

FOREWORD

O OBSERVE THE COLLECTED WORK of Hank Schubart is in no small part to witness the thoughtful expression of locale. The topography of Salt Spring Island itself provides an insistent theme and provides measure to the houses and their sitings. Insofar as each of Schubart's houses responds directly to its conditions of locale, the collective identity of the work offers compelling testimony to architecture's ability to be infused by a broad sense of place. In this respect, we might think of the designs as qualifying the inherited experience of landscape as it is made habitable and rendered for us as home.

In a place such as Salt Spring Island, homes declare their preoccupation with issues of terrain and orientation, yet this urge often presents curious contradictions. The direction of the most extravagant ocean views may also be the source of the most extravagant winter storms—the desire for view might well be at odds with the need for the light and warmth of the sun, and the desire for proximity to the ocean may result in the need for precipitous structural foundations. It is precisely in the reconciliation of such contradictory facts that Schubart's most demonstrable design strength lies, and it is in the houses' common sense of ease that his success is so clearly demonstrated.

DESIGN TACTICS

In their special regard for the attributes of Salt Spring settings, Schubart's houses exhibit a number of specific architectural tactics.

First, there is the consistent development of a skewed and room-deep plan-form, most generally lodged in parallel with the natural contours of the site and acknowledging specific visual attributes of both local and distant landscapes. These sometimes extremely narrow configurations promote cross-ventilation, establish that most fundamental necessity of creating level

Gold house, entrance.

FACING: Gold house, interior living room. ABOVE: Southend house, exterior and pool. BELOW: Gordon-Sumpton house, courtyard entrance.

"ground," and register the relatively short structural spans of conventional wood framing. Even more significantly, these attenuated interior spaces serve as a kind of spatial lens through which the broader landscape can be observed.

The Gold house offers an especially vivid instance of this approach. Approached from an upper-level access road, the roof itself contributes to the primary presentation of the house, granting virtually no awareness of the adjacent waterfront. The rugged forest terrain is drawn into submission, sheltered under deep, projecting eaves. From this point of arrival, entry to the house immediately provides a deliberately framed view of the ocean landscape beyond, relieving the relatively dark and contained space of the forest and reconciling the house's undulating geometric order with the clear mandate of prospect.

Given the local topography and the compelling desire for a house whose experience culminates in a dramatic view, a narrow and meandering Schubart house almost inevitably results in conditions in which the "front" and "back" of the house enjoy radically different prospects. Typically entered through a carefully orchestrated sequence of pathways from higher ground, such a house might confront a steep rock outcrop on its entry side while enjoying a vertiginous drop to the shorefront and ocean only a room's depth away. In addition—and notwithstanding the house's general narrowness—the woodland shade on its perimeter encourages the inclusion of skylit interior spaces that are open to the sky, a feature especially welcome during the often overcast winter days.

In the Southend house, an "uphill" landscape has been orchestrated in which a necessarily narrow pool and surrounding wooden deck are dramatically poised between the house and an outcrop of rock and arbutus trees. This kind of landscape is often coordinated with the passage from forest to interior, providing a sheltered local ecology that might vary dramatically from the exposed elevations facing the water. An excellent example of this is in the case of the Gordon-Sumpton house, where a carefully scaled outdoor living room enjoys a protected southern aspect clearly distinguished from its surroundings.

While these often dramatic juxtapositions of domestic interiors and the extreme geography of their surroundings occur across the collected works of Schubart, his designs almost always take care to draw the interior realm out into adjacent landscape spaces. Enclosed courtyards and, especially, elevated

Pickering cottage, exterior bridge to entrance.

decks extend the utility of interiors but also mitigate the extreme shift in scale between domestic furnishings and the extraordinary natural surroundings. More specifically, these external spaces often acknowledge very specific conditions of orientation and terrain—an unusual rock outcrop or a distinguished tree, for instance. The courtyard that serves as a threshold of arrival also serves as an outdoor living space, bathed in afternoon light and protected from the vigorous and bracing breezes off the water. Similarly but more reservedly, his work uses the extension of primary roof forms to offer both literal and conceptual shelter on arrival.

The often wayward, oblique passages of arrival provide an important threshold and transition between the extravagant scale of the coastal forest and the often quite modest interior domains of the houses. Whether on the bridge leading to the Pickering cottage, or the extended forecourt of the Anstine house, these sequences are crucial in framing the interior experience of each house. This condition is perhaps most pronounced in Schubart's own

Anstine house, entrance.

Schubart house, exterior courtyard entrance.

house, where the downward trajectory of approach is tangent to a contained kitchen garden of fruit trees, vegetables, and herbs—again, a landscape illuminated by a southern exposure and protected from ocean winds. The Schubart house—perhaps not surprisingly—suggests the potential of the house interior to qualify distinct landscapes while offering its own contours of support for the varied tasks of domestic life.

LOCAL CULTURE

The strength of the designs in connecting domestic life to surrounding landscapes—both received and invented—remains a key accomplishment of Schubart's Salt Spring career. It is also interesting to compare Schubart's work to other regional architects' efforts in similar Gulf Island landscapes. While buildings since Schubart's career have often indulged in a scale and level of creature comfort little removed from that of conventional mainland suburban houses, there is a strong tradition in the region of executing materially modest houses while maintaining a finely resolved regard for a site and for inventive material detail.

The modesty of all of these houses derives to some degree from many having been built for secondary, recreational purposes. More critical are the energy and costs associated with bringing building materials to relatively remote sites and the relatively expedient building traditions that often prevail in these settings. A predominant allegiance to vernacular forms flows directly from the use of conventional wood-frame building techniques, although in the case of architect-designed homes, the vernacular is certainly tempered by more self-conscious stylistic influences.

Certainly, the strong influence of Frank Lloyd Wright may be noted in various local practitioners' designs, even without the direct contact that is lodged in Schubart's own personal history. It is worth noting, however, that Wright was profoundly influenced by his own experience of Japanese architecture and, in particular, by his observations of the formal patterns of traditional Japanese houses. The use of deep, projecting eaves and an expressive timber frame resonates with the Japanese cultural heritage as much as it evokes

Schubart house, exterior waterside deck.

XVI Wright's Prairie-style houses. Indeed, these formal references reside very comfortably in the misty evergreen landscapes that typify North America's Pacific Northwest.

During the postwar era of economic affluence and increasing cultural confidence, Canada's West Coast milieu fostered a distinctly regional modernism in architecture, with conspicuous similarities to Schubart's own expressive idiom. The work of architects such as Barry Downs and Paul Merrick—more or less contemporaries of Schubart—shares something of Schubart's sensibility, extending the sense of a local culture informed by geography as much as by history.

ALTERNATIVE PRACTICE

Such examples locate Schubart firmly within the Wrightian conventions of the architectural profession and its valorization of the forceful and expressive individual. However, his political views, personal life, and professional work suggest another cultural tradition and a rather different set of design values. Within the traditions of timber construction—whether designed by the architect or lived by the carpenter—the elaboration and deliberate detailing of elements of structure, enclosure, and interior fixtures draw on the Arts and Crafts movement of Victorian England and its important demonstration in early twentieth-century California. The "craftsman bungalow" as a distinct residential motif was widely executed in British Columbia settlements and maintains a cachet still very apparent in contemporary house building throughout the region.

This tradition, in particular, places emphasis upon the physical logics of construction. In timber-framed practice, this emphasis is most often revealed in the hierarchy of overlaid components of structure—roofing on decking on purlins on rafters on beams carried to columns, for instance—and throughout Schubart's work there is evidence of his ongoing inquiry into the expressive potential of these technical arrangements.

In the Gulf Islands, such a resort to the expressive exuberance of the builder was interestingly reinforced and modified during the era of Schubart's practice by the deliberate pastoralism and self-reliant code of "alternative"

Morningside Organic Bakery Café & Bookstore, exterior detail. © Christopher Macdonald.

culture. Here a piece of driftwood discovered on the beach might be commandeered to serve as the ridge beam of a modest dwelling, and recycled materials might be more generally collaged into the composition of house construction. This "woodbutcher's art" was generally deployed by owner-designer-builders, with varying degrees of finesse. A contemporary project for a local bakery at Fulford Harbour by Everest MacDonald's practice, "Elevation Studios," bears witness to the persisting allure of this kind of local improvisation.

While such an ethos was widespread throughout the Gulf Islands—providing a contemporary version of what was, after all, a tradition of pioneer expediency—it reached a particular and noteworthy level of accomplishment on Hornby Island, some one hundred miles north of Salt Spring. Here, in an even more remote location and beyond the jurisdiction of building regulations, houses of considerable complexity and invention appeared in some abundance, and a culture of thoughtful design and building was begun.

Architects such as Woodruf "Bud" Wood and Michael McNamara, and builders such as Lloyd House, created improvised houses that garnered international attention. The ethos of "hand-built Hornby Island" was acknowledged in a full issue of the London-based journal *Architectural Design* in 1978 and has been projected into contemporary practice most explicitly by Helliwell + Smith Blue Sky Architecture. As the houses became more complex in organization and larger in scale, they assumed a more conventional relationship between owners and designers, yet still emphasized the crucial affiliation between designer and builder that was Schubart's legacy.

In Blue Sky's Shalkai house, many of Schubart's planning tactics may be recognized. Similarly, by working closely with the client, the site, and especially the capacity of the builder, Blue Sky was able to transform Schubart's orthodox roof profiles and accompanying canted plans into a more fluid and sinuous form. The enhanced skills of a subsequent generation of island builders, allied to a very different degree of material modesty, provide the underpinnings to architectural invention of this order, and it is worth noting that Blue Sky acknowledges the debt owed to the early training of its favored builders through their work with Schubart.

Shalkai house, exterior front. © Blue Sky Architecture. Courtesy of the owner.

In keeping with this strain of alternative culture within the Gulf Islands—which is evident in music, literature, and other creative activities—the islands have maintained their position as a place of architectural experimentation and discovery. Even when collaborating with more metropolitan practices, such as Patkau Architects or Battersby + Howat—both in Vancouver—homeowners on Salt Spring and elsewhere continue to use the extraordinary geographical setting to establish ambitious circumstances for their designers. Therefore, Schubart claims a significant historical position in what may be understood as a regional laboratory for domestic architectural invention.

SITUATED MODERNISM

Suggesting a resonance between the work of Schubart and other architects practicing in the region certainly does not challenge the more direct link observed between his work and that of the generation of Bay Area practitioners who inherited the inspiration of William Wurster's important designs and teaching. While projects such as Moore Lyndon Turnbull Whitaker's Sea Ranch were initially positioned within contemporary critical discussion as evidence of a postmodern impulse in American architecture, in retrospect it could be argued that it is their respect for the potential of ordinary construction to be rendered sublime that holds a more enduring interest. It is in this sense that their work engages traditions of modernity alongside those of vernacular practice—in each case, seeking a material culture in which individual expression is committed to collective ideals of social formation and localized concerns for place.

Common to all of these disparate designers was the belief that an experience entirely unprecedented could be constructed out of the most conventional and deeply familiar materials and, further, that such an experience could profoundly refresh our understanding of locale and domestic life. It is within this transformative potential that the best of Schubart's work exists, reminding us, once again, of the capacity for eloquence evident in the everyday.

CHRISTOPHER MACDONALD, Professor of Architecture, School of Architecture and Landscape Architecture, University of British Columbia, FRAIC

PREFACE

 HEN THE ARCHITECT HENRY A. SCHUBART, JR., known as "Hank," moved his family in 1968 to Salt Spring Island in British Columbia, Canada, the island was akin to an outpost today in Alaska or Newfoundland. It had not yet become a retirement destination or earned its reputation as a home to skilled artisans. At the time, the Schubart family was living in San Francisco, and with five teenage sons, their political objections to the Vietnam War had taken on personal urgency. Canada offered them a haven. Just as importantly, the island beckoned Schubart professionally at a moment when he was seeking to work in a community where his creative practice would make a difference.

Before his arrival, architecture on the island had been regarded merely as shelter. Houses were built close to roads, away from the perils of the water's edge, and lots were cut clear of trees in order to minimize damage during winter windstorms. In contrast, Schubart introduced a vision of living that was not simply utilitarian, and refined that sensibility during his thirty years on Salt Spring Island. His work was respectful of local natural materials, economical in presentation, and suffused with light. His designs were precise, elegant, and uncluttered. Very little was done for effect alone. The results are honest structures that respect their surroundings. And the Schubart sensibility lives in features recognizable from house to house. Skylights, for instance, allow natural light to temper British Columbia's long, overcast winters. Most importantly, he was regarded as a genius for finding the perfect site for a house, and some clients hired him solely for that skill. In the end, it was his pragmatism and his "conversation" with his clients that gave his houses their warmth, livability, and elegance.

This book is an introduction to Hank Schubart. His early path took him to Taliesin, back to New York as a draftsman, on to California, and, finally, to Salt Spring Island. He arrived on the island uncertain of how to earn a living but intending to build houses for himself and for others. At his death, in 1998, his legacy included more than 230 projects on the island, of which at least 150 were significant and supervised to completion by him. Most of these were residential projects, but there were also commercial, educational, and religious projects; the majority of these projects continue to populate the landscape. His early involvement in community planning helped focus commercial growth in the island's three towns and thus maintain its rural nature.

Many of his houses were built with modest budgets, but a few can be considered lavish, given their volume and extensive use of natural materials. In other cases, he remodeled existing structures, leaving his fingerprints in the trim details, skylights, broad panes of glass, and decks. Some clients hired him only to site their houses, recognizing their own limited appetite for his tendency to dominate every project element. In commenting on his work, he would simply state: "I have a certain curiosity and love of nature and love of art and love of music. I have no interest in retirement. I expect to work until they cart me away. I like it."[1] Undetectable from the road, Schubart-designed houses inspire strong reactions from the people who live in them, and even stronger reactions about the architect who designed them. Precise addresses have been omitted to protect the occupants; these houses are privately owned.

A declaration of interest is due here: I live in one of his houses. "It's a Schubart," the real estate agent announced when showing the house. For me, this book has been a new kind of project. I am neither an architect nor a biographer—most of my prior writing has been confined to legal memoranda. But once I knew of Schubart, I wanted to know more about this architect who designed my house, with its low profile, large eaves, and fragrance of aged cedar. Schubart oriented the house—"broke the spine" as he would have said—to take full advantage of the views. He separated the large glass panes with cedar mullions in order to bring in nature's art, the trees, water, and outdoors. This project began as a way to introduce the larger world to Schubart's work on Salt Spring Island. In return, I have been introduced to an extraordinary man.

The book is arranged chronologically, and where possible, I have used his own words to describe his working philosophy. He kept nearly all correspondence and files, and those files were a valuable research resource; in other cases, interviews with clients, contractors, family members, and colleagues were used to fill in a portrait of the man and his work. Just as importantly, I wanted to provide a context for his houses. His professional life intersected with the creation of the architectural style known as West Coast modern, and it is within that framework that the homes on Salt Spring Island were designed. Finally, I tried to convey a sense of the personal architectural vocabulary that Schubart used in creating these houses.

I am not certain what Hank Schubart would have thought of a book about his work on Salt Spring Island. I imagine he would have been charming and noncommittal, offering both limited resistance and limited access. He might have responded by declaring his philosophy on residential homes: "I have two great concerns when it comes to designing a home. That it is carefully and beautifully related to the land and that each house represents the needs of the client."[2] Or he might have shared his early work history, making sure I knew that he had worked in New York with Ed Stone on the Museum of Modern Art building and with Jose Sert. He would have mentioned the lessons he took from his days at Wurster Bernardi & Emmons as chief draftsman and how Wurster's love of residential work inspired him. And he certainly would have brought up his year at Taliesin with Frank Lloyd Wright and reflected on Wright's influence. It was, after all, his time at Taliesin that attracted him to architecture as a career. In an interview with the Frank Lloyd Wright Archives at Taliesin West years later, he reflected: "I watched Mr. Wright do the drawings for the Willey House . . . And I watched him work and it was a marvelous experience because it was obvious that the house was all there in his head and it was coming out of his hands." Schubart had been trained as an artist, and this chance to observe a master drawing by hand moved him deeply.

The houses selected for inclusion reflect Schubart's remarkable style and include his favorites. One book cannot address all his many accomplishments; this book is just an introduction to Hank Schubart and his work. Asked by a client to describe his architecture, Schubart reportedly replied, "Glass and cedar, West Coast style, contemporary West Coast style." It was more than cedar and glass: he had been present at the creation of the language of modernism in California, and by the time he arrived on Salt Spring Island, his mastery of it allowed him to control all the details of his projects. Other architects might use the same materials, but they could not fully replicate his vocabulary. Without Hank Schubart there would still be a Salt Spring Island, but it would be a different kind of place.

ACKNOWLEDGMENTS

HIS BOOK HAS BENEFITED GREATLY from the participation of several people who contributed to its narrative and form. First and foremost, I am indebted to members of Hank Schubart's family, particularly Maggie Schubart, who opened her remarkable mind and heart to us. Every visit with her was a lesson in how to age undaunted, and her light but formidable fingerprints gave this book its full form. The Schubart family's willingness to share memories, files, and insights brought the man into clearer focus. Second, I am grateful to the homeowners who so graciously opened their doors and to Schubart's contractors, professional colleagues, and friends who shared their memories for this project. Together, their candor and humor added valuable dimensions and insights. Robert Barnard was very generous in sharing both the Schubart file archives and his perspective on Hank as an architect.

This book would not have found a home at the University of Texas Press without the encouragement, guidance, and steady hand of Jim Burr. He was responsive, knowledgeable, and affirming over the many years during which this project took form. His initial curiosity in Schubart's work made me think that this book might have a broader audience than I had originally contemplated. I am deeply grateful that this project, and this author, ended up in his experienced hands. One of Joanna Hitchcock's legacies at the press will be the depth and tenor of the staff she built, and I am very appreciative of her leadership there and of the press's staff.

Schubart did not document his work through photographs. Doing justice to Schubart's work required a skilled photographer, and Jim Alinder's photography captured the beauty of the architecture and gave the project clearer direction. He is a natural teacher, and the book's beauty owes much to him. Pirkle Jones, the photographer, documented his home when it was built, and he photographed other California works by Schubart. These 1960s black-and-white photographs are included in the book. Jones's professional regard and personal fondness for Hank prompted him to entrust his memories and his remarkable photographs, and I am grateful that we were able to include his perspective and art. Thanks also go to Jennifer McFarland for making these prints possible and for granting me access to the Pirkle Jones Foundation, and to Mark Citret for printing and giving new life to old photographs.

I was very fortunate to have two accomplished and prominent architects write for this book: Christopher Macdonald, FRAIC, a professor of architecture at the University of British Columbia's School of Architecture and Landscape Architecture, and Heather McKinney, FAIA, the founding principal of McKinney York Architects. Chris added his academic and architectural perspective and thereby affirmed the value of Schubart's work. His editorial insights, site plans, and encouragement were invaluable, and his Foreword stands alone as an essay on the importance of Schubart's work to the Gulf Islands. Heather has worked with us on multiple projects, and I trust and admire her talent, experience, and perspective. She updated a Schubart home, and her Afterword adds an important dimension to his work. Both essays reflect a generous appreciation of Schubart's architectural skills from accomplished professionals.

Lisa Germany, an architectural writer of some distinction, provided editorial insights as this project took form. She helped refine the book's early scope into a manageable structure that would accommodate a compelling narrative. Others who provided valuable assistance include Cathrine Tait, who added drafting expertise in finalizing the site plans for inclusion in this book; Jonas Dodd, who worked with Chris Macdonald early on in creating the plans; Paul Schubart, who also added drafting expertise in creating the plan for the Schubart home; Lauren Jahnke, who helped bring the final draft into submission form; and Toby Fouks, who spent months over two long winters cataloging Schubart's files and making them accessible and usable—I am particularly thankful for her work. Tania Kingsbury brought her considerable organizational skills to this project. Her help in transcribing notes, formatting the initial submissions, and managing the photo shoots was central to the success of this project; I am grateful to her for all of her contributions. Thanks go also to the

staffs at two research institutions: the Frank Lloyd Wright Archives at Taliesin
West in Scottsdale, Arizona, and the Environmental Design Archives at the
University of California, Berkeley. They graciously offered assistance, access
to files and photographs, and a place to work.

Finally, this book would not have occurred but for the encouragement and
participation of Jane Hickie. I am thankful to her for taking on so many roles in
this project, from co-interviewer to editor to collaborator-in-chief. Without
her, this book, and my life, would not be the same.

MICHELE DUNKERLEY
November 2010

HOUSES

MADE

OF

WOOD

AND

LIGHT

FIRST GLIMPSE

 N MARCH 26, 1968, A COLD, wet day, a Volkswagen van crossed the border from Blaine, Washington, into mainland British Columbia. Driving the van was fifty-two-year-old Hank Schubart, a California architect who, for the prior twenty years, had had an enviable practice in San Francisco. With him were his wife, Maggie, their sons Daniel and Paul, and their young daughter, Gabrielle. Steering closely behind on a three-wheel motorbike was son Matthew. Michael, their second son, was living in Toronto, and their eldest, Peter, was enrolled in school in Santa Cruz, California. Both older sons were of draft age, and the younger three were facing eligibility in the next few years.

This was not Hank Schubart's first visit to the island. That had occurred the year before, when clients commissioned him to build a house there on land bordering the main harbor. When he first saw Salt Spring Island, the rural island was a far cry from his home in San Francisco, which was witnessing the "summer of love," with its psychedelic circus and war protests. For the Schubart family—adamantly opposed to the Vietnam War—life in Canada offered their sons the choice to avoid the draft by becoming Canadian citizens. The decision to move meant a step backward financially, but was regarded within the family as its own "act of love."

For Schubart, there was a simultaneous force at work. Salt Spring, the largest of the Southern Gulf Islands, was a place of such raw beauty and firm character that it held out the promise of a new chance to design the kind of residential architecture his sensibility craved. Located in the Strait of Georgia, a major navigation channel between the coast of British Columbia and Vancouver Island, the island was covered in emerging second-growth forests and populated by hardworking people who farmed, logged, and fished. Its natural borders of mountains and ocean shaped the remote lives of the residents.

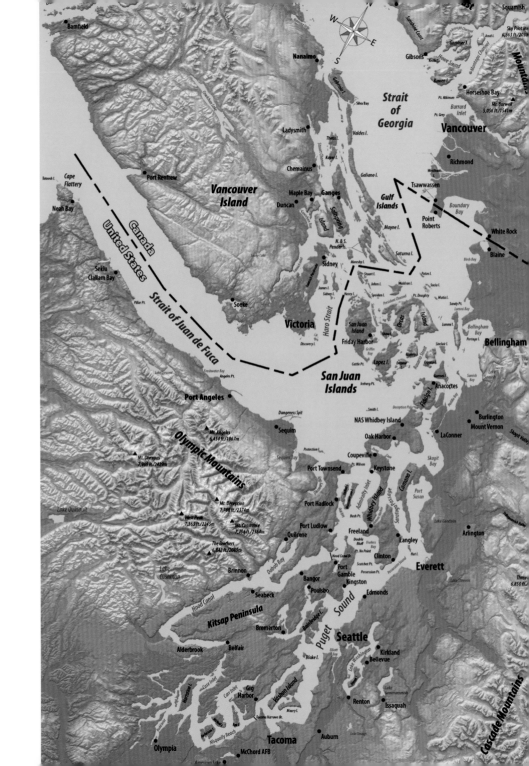

4

The island was framed by small settlements on its north and south ends, and farms and cottages dotted the landscape. The Schubart family's arrival came at the right time for him and for the island, which in the years ahead would try to forge a model of how to encourage development without losing its soul.

In 1968, the island was changing and growing. More frequent ferry crossings and a new Long Harbour terminal connected the island more directly to Vancouver on mainland British Columbia and to nearby Victoria on Vancouver Island. A growing regional economy attracted new residents, some fleeing crowded metropolitan areas, some seeking a warmer place in which to retire or pursue a simpler life, and some, like the Schubart family, driven north from the United States by the Vietnam War. Upon arrival, the Schubart family found a hospital, a grocery store, a general store, schools, and a few basic services.

The island's official population in 1968 was about two thousand full-time residents, and no one could have predicted that it would grow to more than ten thousand by the time Schubart died, thirty years later. It is a wonder that when he first saw the island, he knew that it offered him a place to create the kind of architecture that would respond to its surroundings in an endless conversation. But that is jumping ahead of the story.

PERSONAL HISTORY: NEW YORK TO PARIS AND BACK

A continent away, far from the wild beauty of British Columbia, Henry Allen Schubart, Jr., called "Hank," was born in New York City on August 15, 1916, the first of two sons born to Pauline (Werner) and Henry Schubart, Sr. His early years were comfortable; the family had an apartment in New York City and spent weekends and summers on their farm, Chumleigh, in Ossining, New York. Hank's father was a businessman and cotton broker whose financial acumen helped preserve the family's wealth through the 1929 stock market crash. His mother was an artist who, rare for the time, held both a bachelor's degree from Smith College as well as a master's in social work from Barnard College (Columbia University). Although Hank's father had little time for social activism, his mother's involvement in social and political matters, including public housing, instilled in her eldest son a lifelong determination to make a difference. Pauline Schubart's father, a graduate of the City College of

FACING: Topographical Map of the U.S. San Juan Islands and Canadian Gulf Islands. © 2010 Kenmore Air Harbor, Inc. Topographical data courtesy of True North GIS. Courtesy of Kenmore Air, the seaplane airline.

6   New York, had been an influential lawyer and a Hebrew scholar. Still, according to Hank, it was not his grandparents' accomplishments that impressed him as a child. Instead, he remembered "that Grandpa Werner always had turkey gravy on the napkin that he tucked under his chin at Thanksgiving family dinners, which always were good big feeds and at which brother Mickey and I sneaked out to the carpeted big front hall where we had fun goosing a white marble Greek statue of the Venus de Milo."[1]

His privileged background enabled Hank to attend private schools in New York City, including the Horace Mann School. When he was thirteen and his brother Mark was eleven, the family moved to Europe.

Although Henry Sr. had managed to avoid the stock market crash of 1929, friends had not. For two years, Henry Sr. took frequent trips back to the United States to help the widow of a less fortunate friend while his family lived in France. But the Schubart boys were unconcerned with such weighty worldly matters, attending the Lycée d'Antibes on the beautiful Côte D'Azur. Hank then enrolled for a year at the Académie Julian in Paris, taking design courses at the École des Beaux-Arts. He threw himself into painting and drawing, adding anatomy classes to bolster his drawing skills. His fluency in French remained for the rest of his life, and from that young age, he and his brother always conversed in French. If the trip marked the beginning of a new chapter in Hank's life, it also marked an end: at fifteen, Hank's formal schooling came to a close. That was not the end of his education, however, and with his parents' acquiescence, he enrolled in art school to become a painter. The effects of this decision would resonate later in life, particularly when he sought professional licenses to practice architecture.

Hank's time in Paris produced friendships and professional associations that would last long into his adult years. For example, Martin Baer, with whom he studied in Paris, became a lifelong friend. In Paris, he was a student of the artists Egon von Vietinghoff and Alexander Archipenko, and Hank continued to study sculpture with Archipenko after his return to New York. Although he would follow an architectural path in the years ahead, these early experiences of studying art in France remained important to him. His training as a young art student taught him to see and laid the foundation for the freehand drawings he used throughout his career.

In 1932, with the world still mired in the Great Depression, the Schubart family returned from France and settled into their pattern of spending weekdays in New York and weekends on Chumleigh Farm. At Chumleigh, Pauline and Henry Sr. allowed Hank to remodel the second story of the main house to use as his art studio. But the familiar family routine was not to last; shortly after the return to New York, Henry Sr. told Pauline that he was leaving her and the boys to marry his friend's widow, Fanny Kilburn, the source of his frequent trips back to New York. For the next several years, problems surrounding his parents' divorce consumed Hank's family time and altered his relationship with his father. Laying the blame for his parents' divorce squarely at the feet of Henry Sr., Hank gave his allegiance to his mother and dealt his father out of the family deck. For months after the divorce, Hank avoided speaking to his father, and for years he refused to ask him for money for living or educational expenses, though the two did eventually reestablish ties.

With the self-confidence of a favored son, Hank set out to find his own path. Nearing his sixteenth birthday, while his peers were contemplating college, Hank searched for a profession. He enjoyed physical labor, craftsmanship, and art, activities far removed from his father's business practices. Pauline encouraged her son's artistic interests. In fact, both Schubart boys would go on to have careers in the arts: Hank in the visual arts and architecture, and his younger brother, Mark, in music.[2] The turning point for Hank came when his mother's sister, Adelaide Werner, bought him a copy of Frank Lloyd Wright's *An Autobiography*. As he later recalled, "That's what started the whole thing as far as Taliesin was concerned."[3] This book was an account of Wright's work, personal life, and philosophical approach to architecture. Published when Wright was a well-known public figure, it was revealing, charming, and audacious, and it captivated Hank at an impressionable time. When he happened upon a *New York Times* article about the newly established Taliesin Fellowship, Hank, then sixteen, began to think of applying.

WRIGHT WAS SIXTY-THREE YEARS OLD WHEN HIS THIRD WIFE, Olgivanna, suggested that they found a school for educating young architects. This idea, which came at a low point in Wright's career—the Great Depression had had a devastating impact on architecture generally—proved inspiring. The original prospectus outlining the fellowship was published in October 1932, and the newspaper article describing it enthralled Schubart. The fellowship was to be an apprenticeship program in architecture as well as in music, sculpture, and painting.[4] The apprentices, up to seventy-seven in number, would live and work on Wright's family farm, Taliesin, located on 200 acres of pastures in southwestern Wisconsin, near the town of Spring Green.

Hank found the promise of a collective teaching experience alluring. It was clear that, for him, the solitary life of a painter was not appealing: he sought a wider range of experience, something that would combine a creative life with that of building trades. On August 20, 1932, Hank sent Wright a letter, introducing himself and inquiring about the requirements for admission. Writing on Chumleigh Farm stationery, he described himself as fluent in French and as someone who enjoyed both painting ("my life work!") and physical labor. With its call for architecture combined with craftsmanship, gardening, carpentry, and general physical labor, the description of Taliesin as a "bookless school" was, for the young Schubart, "like a dream come true." He continued, "Two months ago having read your autobiography very eagerly I found in you a man of my ideals and a sympathetic and understanding individual so that writing to you and asking whether I might be able to share this beautiful venture, thrills me. If you feel that I am worthwhile material for your fellowship I would like to know more about it."[5]

Despite being designated a "fellowship," the program at Taliesin required students to pay tuition, and Henry Sr. did not support his son's desire to attend. Hank was undeterred. He spent the next year in New York and wrote again in 1933, asking about admission requirements that fall, particularly regarding any minimum age or educational requirements. Within a week, Schubart had a response. Karl Jensen, the secretary of the Taliesin Fellowship, informed him that a new fellowship prospectus was being prepared and would be mailed soon. He offered that a Mr. Churchill, in New York, was familiar with Taliesin and could advise Schubart about the program: "You will find in the new prospectus that the tuition has been raised from $675 to $1100 for the year. There are no requirements as to age nor formal education—although most of our apprentices are post-graduate from various universities. The requirement necessary is a desire to come under the conditions of the prospectus which has been changed considerably from the one you have."[6]

The changed prospectus called for a much more informal structure for the fellowship. Enrollment was limited to twenty-three apprentices, but the three basic elements of a Taliesin education remained: first, training in drafting skills by assisting with Wright's architectural work; second, learning building techniques and construction methods by framing, modifying, repairing, and remodeling Taliesin; and, finally, acquiring the knowledge of how to maintain buildings, make minor repairs, and support the daily routine at Taliesin, which included cooking, gardening, laundry, and all the other work required to maintain a life without servants.[7]

Hank acted without hesitation. He wrote to Wright that he would like to come and stay with him for a while. He wrote of having cooked, painted, and done all kinds of hard work on the family farm. Wright wrote back: "Come ahead."[8]

CHAPTER 2

WRIGHT'S TALIESIN

"THE MOST INFORMING EXPERIENCE OF MY LIFE"

O N SEPTEMBER 8, 1933, Schubart set out for Taliesin, stopping first to visit the 1933 World's Fair in Chicago. With no means of support, he traveled by train with friends, at times hopping rides both for adventure and out of necessity. From Chicago, Schubart sent a telegram to Taliesin, announcing his imminent arrival in Spring Green, Wisconsin. He walked from the Spring Green railroad station and knocked on Taliesin's door. Frank Lloyd Wright opened the door and asked who he was. Schubart introduced himself, and Wright responded, "Well, come on in and we'll give you a room."[1]

However confident he was, Hank was only seventeen when he settled into Taliesin that fall, and by his own admission, his connection to architecture at that point was more romantic than practical. Most of the other Taliesin apprentices were in their twenties, college graduates, and even graduates of architecture school.[2]

These circumstances made Schubart's easy acceptance into the fellowship somewhat curious. Wright expected the apprentices to shoulder all manner of chores at Taliesin—cooking meals, constructing buildings, doing masonry and carpentry—as well as pay their tuition. Schubart was a willing laborer and an eager pupil, but never paid tuition. Instead, he worked in exchange for food and whatever training he could pick up. He clearly had a wonderful time. In 1995, Schubart recalled what it was like in those early days at the Taliesin Fellowship:

We spent a lot of time going around scrounging firewood to keep the place warm. It was terribly cold. In fact, one of the memories I have is having my fingers stick to the silver when we set the table for breakfast, because breakfast was early. Those of us who had to get up and bake bread and

FACING: Schubart firing the kiln at Taliesin. Courtesy of the Frank Lloyd Wright Foundation, Taliesin West, Scottsdale, Arizona.

set the table, and get everything organized for the day, usually had to be in the kitchen at 5:30 or 6 o'clock—which, in Wisconsin, in the middle of winter when it's thirty or forty below, is *cold*. They didn't have the money to properly heat or run the boilers or anything. We were sort of general laborers, did whatever we had to turn our hand to. During the summer, of course, we worked in the fields hoeing corn and picking fruit—just on the farm. I really liked that and always have.[3]

Opportunities to observe Wright at work were rare. There were lectures and discussions, but Taliesin was not a working studio during the early 1930s. The apprentices saw Wright regularly when he rose early in the morning to play the piano or work in the garden. Although several large projects in the office had been shelved after the economy collapsed—a luxurious hotel in Arizona, an apartment building, a school in California, and apartment towers in New York and Chicago—toward the end of 1933, two important works, the Johnson Wax Building and the innovative Broadacre City plan, were initiated. Schubart was given the opportunity to help build the models for Broadacre City, and when Wright received the commission for the Willey house in Minneapolis, he finally had the opportunity to observe Wright at work on a residential project. By his own admission, Schubart lacked the skill to produce architectural drawings; he remembered being awestruck as he watched Wright draw the plans for the Willey house project: "I've never forgotten because he started at one corner of the board and he composed it the way you almost do a free-hand drawing—with a T-square and triangle. And I watched him work and it was a marvelous experience because it was obvious that the house was all there in his head and it was coming out of his hands. That was a very moving experience."[4]

The dire economic times did not halt all activity at Taliesin; Schubart and the other apprentices were busy constructing and maintaining buildings, including the Taliesin Playhouse, which was opened in November 1933 as an integral part of Wright's program. Outsiders (occasionally from Spring Green) were invited to attend live performances and films on Sundays. The playhouse was to assume a role in Hank's relationship not only with Wright but also with Henry Schubart, Sr. Wright supposed that Hank's father could afford

Taliesin as Schubart experienced it in 1933–1934. Courtesy of the Frank Lloyd Wright Foundation, Taliesin West, Scottsdale, Arizona.

Schubart engaged in stonework at Taliesin. Courtesy of the Frank Lloyd Wright Foundation, Taliesin West, Scottsdale, Arizona.

to purchase a piano for the playhouse, and not just any piano, but a concert grand. While Hank was at home in New York during the holidays, he approached his father with Wright's request that he pay for a piano. Hank then reported to Wright that his father might join forces with two other parents to purchase the piano. Writing to Henry Sr. in February 1934, Wright pursued the piano campaign. Interestingly, this letter also includes words that were an accurate prediction of Hank's future ("He will do good work someday"), but a future that was far from obvious at that moment. One picks up also the persuasive voice of Wright trying to soften up a prospective patron.

> My dear Mr. Schubart:
>
> The piano matter comes in sight again . . . At the moment we are in need of money and we have to fight the cold and keep going. Mr. Tafel has been trying to raise a little money for us and I have no doubt Mr. Bush would do the same thing. So if you can get together and send us this piano "toute suite" it will give our work an impetus we need . . .
>
> Henry is a good boy and keeping fit. He will do good work someday. My best to you and Mrs. Schubart.
>
> Sincerely yours,
> Frank Lloyd Wright
> Taliesin: Spring Green: Wisconsin: February 26, 1934[5]

Henry Sr. refused this request from Wright, and one of the other parents eventually stepped in. Schubart recalled, "I think, finally, Alfie Bush's father furnished the piano. It was a Bechstein. It was absolutely beautiful."[6]

"AT TALIESIN"

After being recalled to New York for a brief family emergency in the spring of 1934, Schubart traveled back to Wisconsin for the remainder of the spring and summer months. Schubart's return to Taliesin coincided with Wright's expanding efforts to market himself to a broader audience. Newspaper columns written by Wright, by apprentices, and even by guests were published in several southern Wisconsin newspapers under the title "At Taliesin." Schubart collaborated on a few of these columns, preparing drafts for Wright's editorial pen.[7]

About this time, Schubart's mother began to develop her own relationship with Frank Lloyd Wright. Pauline Schubart initially thought that Taliesin was a school where her son could follow a conventional curriculum and complete his formal education. Even after she recognized that was not the case, she endorsed Hank's stay there and saw it as beneficial for his future interests. "There is no doubt about Taliesin in being the best place for him," she wrote to Wright in March 1934. "He is part of it in every fibre of his being and your inspirational guidance is everything to him."[8] She traveled to Taliesin later that year, intent on nursing her son after he broke his leg in a buggy accident. While there, Wright invited her to be a guest columnist for "At Taliesin." She became a wholehearted convert to the Taliesin program, writing about the value of the real-life lessons the apprentices were experiencing by living in a home, not an institution. Having to clean, cook, wash dishes, repair and build structures, and decorate a home would, she wrote, enhance the apprentices' creativity and architectural perspective. She praised a crucial lesson her son was taking from his time at Taliesin:

> Having known all the intimate details of this kind of living, they can never again regard a house as just so much material put together. They will be aware that people are moving about in it, leaning on it, so to speak, for moral support. It must become part of their aesthetic life as well as fulfilling the roles of privacy, expediency and convenience. Therefore the house they build for people to live in will be a home rather than a house. I am convinced that they will find some way to make whatever building they do home building rather than house building.[9]

The lessons that Schubart was learning moved beyond building and drafting plans to a philosophy of living. Still, for all his experiences and seeming independence, Hank remained immature and even feckless. He had a cocky confidence that everything would just fall into place. Although he knew that Wright strongly disapproved of students driving to Spring Green for meals or drinking, he and his friends did so fairly regularly, buying corn whiskey from local farmers and even ducking out for breakfast. Wright, greatly annoyed, caught Schubart a few times and threatened to send him back to New York. Wright recalled these youthful antics the next year when Schubart asked to return for a second year at Taliesin.[10]

In August 1934, just after his eighteenth birthday, Schubart abruptly left Taliesin to work at an archaeological site in Iraq. The Joint Assyrian Expedition needed a draftsman, artist, and surveyor on an expedition in Mosul, Iraq, sponsored by the American Schools of Oriental Research (and the University of Pennsylvania), and Schubart secured the job with the help of another Taliesin apprentice, Paul Beidler. Without saying good-bye to Wright, Schubart left to join the expedition, writing only after realizing his rudeness. In his letter, Hank tried to keep the door open for a return to Taliesin, insisting that if Wright wanted him to return, he would gladly do so. In addition, Schubart reflected on his time at Taliesin and his plans for the future:

> I am sincerely hoping that you would understand our having left without having said the customary goodbyes. Goodbys [sic] are usually very banal and we did cover all the ground in our talk we had last week. I hope it is not goodbye Mr. Wright, because if you still want me to come back next spring I will leap gladly at the opportunity.
>
> I was planning to take you to the train the morning you left and would have made my adieux at that time but you requested that Jim take you in the Cord. I completely forgot that you wouldn't be back before our departure.
>
> I cannot possibly say all that I would like to in regard to my year at Taliesin . . . If a success so much the better; if a failure, it has been a very very happy one. After this respite, I hope to return and make the failure a success.
>
> As you probably know, I am going to spend some time in New York before sailing, and if possible, will wheedle a very rich uncle who might, in a moment of forgetfulness, donate some money to the very finest venture in the world today. I'm so attached to Taliesin and to you and Mrs. Wright, that I would do all within my power to give it a helping hand. I'm going to miss you all very badly [and] will await the day when I can come back and resume my life with you all.

I promise to keep in touch with you and let you know how the work turns out at the dig, and if finances allow will send you something in the way of Oriental culture from Iraq. Will also keep my eyes open for ideas that would be useful to you and the Fellowship. My love to you all and best of luck until my return.[11]

THE EXPEDITION

By late 1934, Schubart was settled into the expedition's routine. Over the course of a few months, his work took him to Syria, Turkey, Palestine, and Egypt. In contrast to the camaraderie he had experienced at Taliesin—as he stated in a letter to the Wrights in December 1934—he found himself an outsider, "very much like a dog barking up the wrong tree," with his archaeological colleagues, whom he found constrained by their focus on graves and ancient tablets. He also shared with them his observations on local architecture, noting, "Oh you should see their homes. As regards simplicity in architecture this is the last word, mud, mud bricks, olive branch thatchings, and an innate sense of an organic plan. That's all. Practically no furniture as they sleep, eat, and sit on the floor, a hole in the roof for smoke, and windows. Not luxurious one might say, but with the addition of a chair, a bed and a table they become the most restful and livable rooms."[12]

Schubart's time in Iraq on the expedition seemed to cement his desire to return to Taliesin, and he began a campaign to persuade Wright that he had matured. The pace of life in nearby cities had not tempted him, he reported, so he stayed instead in the countryside near the dig. Mostly, he missed Taliesin and the fellowship:

My work is interesting if not a little tedious, but I am really learning to work (if you will believe me) and am enjoying every minute of my time. And I'll not let architecture slip by the boards either . . . When I come back in the spring I'll have a roll of plans for you as well as a lot of sketches that I have made of the various types of native dwellings both here and in Palestine. They make an interesting comparative study. Arabic too is keeping me busy and I find it a beautiful language. Although I have few regrets I sorely miss

Taliesin and there are few days when my thoughts are not with the Fellowship most of the time. I am that way though and usually want what I can't have at the moment.[13]

Pauline Schubart began her own crusade on behalf of her son. Writing to Wright in January 1935, she noted that Hank was having an interesting experience, but "the inspirational and adventurous joy of new discoveries which filled his life with you" was lacking.

RETURNING HOME

Schubart returned home with a desire to resume work for Wright, but the ground under his Taliesin foundation had shifted. Although he had been only too glad to work in any capacity and to watch Wright design without paying tuition, that opportunity was now closed to him. In later years, Schubart explained that it was because he was "headstrong and opinionated and difficult."

> I'm a very anti-institution person and always have been. In that sense, Mr. Wright liked to control the situation and have the students gather around him. I guess maybe that was sort of like my revolt against my father and a lot of institutions of power. I think Mr. Wright sort of resented that in me.[14]

However, when Wright wrote to Schubart in May 1935, he frankly laid out his own concerns and they had little in common with Schubart's perceptions of the situation. Hank's willingness to break the rules had demonstrated a lack of respect for the program and a pronounced immaturity. Moreover, by any estimation, Wright was a towering architectural talent, and Schubart's lack of courtesy by leaving for Iraq without saying good-bye had not gone unnoticed. Wright could have pointed out that Taliesin was not wanting for applicants among aspiring young architects willing to pay tuition, but instead he wrote:

My dear Hank:

I have been in a quandary concerning your return to Taliesin. I want to be fair and frank with you. No one appreciates your good qualities more than I do but your kicking out last fall in the circumstances made me feel I couldn't really depend on you. Your center of gravity shifted too easily. And already I felt that you would be smooth to me to my face and disrespectful behind my back to keep on good terms with your sense of humor.

I have the greatest respect and consideration for your mother and I do not wish to deny that you yourself have considerable ability and winning qualities if only you were trustworthy. You see, we can't live the life we live here so closely in common unless the Fellowships are more carefully chosen than they have been. I've learned a lot about that this past year, as things come to light. Of course you've knocked about the world a lot and contacted probably what I would consider pretty low types of men and women. Your view of life can't fail to be smirched by that. Now I don't care for angels with a lily even in one hand—but neither do I care for equivocal minded pseudo youth—young so far as responsibilities and abilities go and adult so far as attitude and sophistication goes. Your type of sophistication is not the type I want to live with nor desire to encourage in any way.

But you may have changed. Your mother says you have. I don't know why or how but I do know it might be so. Therefore I am unwilling to shut the door in your face even if the work here didn't need money which it does need more uncompromisingly than ever. So all considered I am going to say that if you care to come and try again complying with all the terms of the prospectus on a footing with the group of apprentices who pay full apprenticeship fees I am willing to try again hoping to see you otherwise than I have been seeing you.

However, I am not willing to make you any more financial concessions nor make any more allowances for your "adolescence." If you come in again you will come in as a man with full responsibility and because you want to share this work more than you want anything else, anywhere. No use otherwise as you wouldn't last three months.

Please give my best regards to your mother. I hope your Iraq interlude did something for you that you really needed.

Sincerely yours,
Frank Lloyd Wright[15]

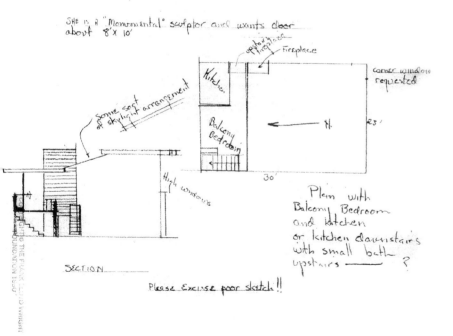

SHE IS A "Monumental" sculptor and wants door about 8' x 10'

Some sort of skylight arrangement

restoration. Fireplace

corner window requested

Kitchen

Balcony Bedroom

N.

High windows

SECTION

30'

Plan with Balcony Bedroom and kitchen or kitchen downstairs with small bath upstairs ———— ?

Please Excuse poor sketch !!

Schubart's rough first architectural drawing, for a sculptor's studio, 1935. Courtesy of the Frank Lloyd Wright Foundation, Taliesin West, Scottsdale, Arizona.

This letter had an effect on Schubart that he would long remember. He wrote back, enthusiastic about rejoining Taliesin, and once again gave Wright assurances that he had matured. In later years, he continued to read something into Wright's letter that had more to do with Schubart's sense of himself than it did with Wright's concerns: "I think the tone of the letter that Mr. Wright wrote when I wanted to come back was sort of an indication that they felt that I had had my experiences in Europe and I was sophisticated. I forget what terms he used. I was a very independent cuss—always have been, for that matter."[16]

Wright's message also concerned tuition, which was $1,100. Schubart Sr. was unable or unwilling to help, and Hank's attempts to collect enough funds by canvassing his relatives fell $400 short, so he could not afford the tuition for fall 1935. Schubart continued to lobby Wright about returning to Taliesin at a reduced tuition, emphasizing that he had matured and that there was nothing more important to him than another year at Taliesin. But Wright held firm for full tuition. Undaunted, Schubart wrote of a potential client—for Wright—whom he had encountered in New York while visiting Rockefeller Center to see the large architectural model of Broadacre City, a planned community.[17] The woman described her plans for a $2,500 studio. Dutifully sending this client to Wright, Schubart enclosed with his note a "quick sketch" to illustrate what the client wanted. This sketch survives as Schubart's earliest architectural drawing.

Schubart spent his days in New York working as a draftsman or a carpenter on occasional small remodeling jobs, adding to his drafting experience. Those were difficult days, as the downcast Schubart wrote to Wright in December 1935: "New York becomes more and more depressing and devitalizing every day." In the letter, he asked whether he, his mother, and another former apprentice, Alfred Bush, might visit Taliesin for a few days and discuss once more the possibility of his returning to the Fellowship. Wright wrote back that Hank and his mother would be welcome for Christmas, but reiterated that Schubart would need to pay full tuition if he wanted to rejoin the group: "As for your staying—I have already put that up to you Hank."[18] Schubart never returned to Taliesin after that holiday visit.

As is often the case with any unfulfilled desire, Schubart's feelings about Taliesin grew in magnitude as time passed. He attended night school for his high school certificate and made a few other small steps that suggest that his "adolescence," as Wright had put it, was waning. For starters, he became more independent, moving from the privileged area of midtown New York that he had known while growing up (and where both his parents lived) to bohemian Greenwich Village, downtown. Then, in 1936, Schubart married Barbara Joseph, who was a few years his senior. He was nineteen years old, short of the legal age to independently marry. The young couple moved to Los Angeles, where Schubart found work as an architectural draftsman for Kistner and Curtis Architects. But this stay was short. The following year, they were back in New York to be closer to their families, because Barbara was expecting their first daughter, Mallory. Two years later, in 1939, a second daughter, Linda, was born.

Back in New York, Schubart found jobs with the architectural firms of Morris Ketchum, Maxfield Vogel, and Van der Gracht and Kilham. He changed jobs frequently, resisting the adjustments demanded by large firms and preferring the flexibility of smaller offices. A stint with Edward D. Stone and Philip Goodwin, notable modern architects, involved Schubart in plans for the Museum of Modern Art building on 53rd Street in Manhattan. Schubart also designed and made models for the 1939 New York World's Fair while working for Stone, most likely including exhibits for the American Association of Railroads and a food pavilion. The work for Stone seemed glamorous, but for Schubart, it was once again an office environment where someone else was in control. Describing it later in life, he said, "I worked for Ed Stone in New York and [for a while] on the Museum of Modern Art building and some of the 1939 World's Fair buildings. I worked with Ed Stone for a year or so. And I found working for other architects very disappointing and very difficult."[19]

His scrambling in and out of architectural drafting jobs added to the pressure of supporting a young family. To help his career, Schubart took a course in structural engineering. His lack of academic credentials, a hindrance in the hierarchical culture of large firms in New York, must have frustrated Schubart's

Hank Schubart with his second wife, Lilo Hemp (Raymond). Courtesy of and copyright by the Estate of Lilo (Hemp) Raymond.

self-confidence. To be licensed as an architect in New York State required the completion of strict academic training and the passing of standardized exams. By 1940, his struggling career was colliding with a failing marriage. His next job, as a draftsman and field supervisor for a homebuilder, Alexander Houses, in New Canaan, Connecticut, disappointed him even more. These were New England tract homes that echoed seventeenth-century Colonial architecture. With their steeply pitched roofs supported by austere and formal façades, the houses were an unpleasant reminder of how far Wright's Taliesin was behind him. He would keep a set of Alexander house plans for years as an example of what not to do in architecture.

When the United States entered World War II, Schubart was twenty-five years old and newly divorced. With two children and an ex-wife to support, he left for Kentucky, working as an electrical draftsman and assistant electrical engineer at a U.S. Navy shipyard. Just before departing from New York, Schubart met Lilo Hemp, a German refugee who had come to the United States in 1939 at age seventeen, and she accompanied him to Louisville.[20] To occupy her time, Schubart bought Hemp her first camera, a Graflex Speed Graphic, a gift that ultimately would set her on her own notable professional path. In 1943, Hank and Lilo married in Louisville. They lived above a garage, and Hank planted a large garden in the lot behind their apartment. When it came time for harvest, it was he who canned vegetables.

It was not a surprise that he joined the U.S. Maritime Service in 1944 as a radio operator. He was twenty-eight, older than other enlistees, but physically fit. He spent all his time stateside during the war. In 1945, he and Lilo returned to New York. But this second marriage was not to last.

Back in New York, without an architecture degree, he could not become a registered architect, and he continued moving from firm to firm. One of his most satisfying jobs was working for the Spanish architect Jose Sert. Paul Wiener and Sert hired Schubart to work on the plan for Motor City near Rio de Janeiro, Brazil, for several months in 1945 (this was a town to be built around an airplane-engine factory). But his experience with Sert stands out among all his work in New York for reasons that were not directly related to architecture.

The first architect who I worked for who I really enjoyed as a person, and his politics and his feeling for life was Jose Sert. I worked for Sert for quite a while in New York after the war. I really enjoyed and felt very warm toward Jose Sert. He was sort of a refugee from the Spanish Civil War and I worked with him on a project in Brazil. He was a very kindly and thoughtful man who—I would say he was not a great architect, but a great man, a nice man.[21]

Sert had impressive modernist credentials as an architect and urban planner, and after he became dean of the Graduate School of Design at Harvard University, he was to influence many young architects. Sert's own work was influenced by the International Style, particularly the ideas of Le Corbusier, which diverged from the warm naturalism of Frank Lloyd Wright's architecture. That alone might have been enough to earn an equivocal judgment from Schubart. Nonetheless, in the years to come, his own style of architecture would resonate with the functionalism that dominated the International Style as he discarded the more decorative elements of traditional houses.

SCHUBART'S ADMIRATION FOR WRIGHT NEVER FLAGGED. Those days at Taliesin made an indelible impression, changing how he looked at architecture, and what he experienced at Taliesin would inform his approach toward architecture for the rest of his life. As he later recalled what it was like:

> I was just awestruck by the architecture of Taliesin. I had been all over Europe and seen all the great cathedrals. I had been in all the great museums and seen the paintings and had loved Europe very much. But nothing touched me as a potential architect the way coming to Taliesin did. It was very extraordinary. Of course, at that point, especially those of us who were brought up in New York and Connecticut, and so on, all were used to living in little boxes with windows. Little old houses. This was a very liberating experience. That's about the best thing I can say for it. I've never changed my feelings for those [Taliesin] buildings. In memory and photographs and everything else, they touch me very much.[22]

CHAPTER 3

THE MAKING OF A WEST COAST MODERNIST

Y 1946, SCHUBART HAD PACKED a lot of experience into a young career. His early efforts at architecture and marriage had resulted in disappointment and frustration. All of that was about to change, however, in the wake of two fateful events: an introduction to Margaret O'Connell, the woman who was to become his lifelong partner, and their decision to move to California.

Margaret O'Connell, known as "Maggie," was a Roman Catholic from Rochester, New York. After graduating from the College of New Rochelle, she moved to New York and eventually become an editor of CBS's radio music programs. Mark Schubart, a professional acquaintance, introduced her to his brother, Hank. Both Hank and Maggie wanted children; Lilo, still seeking her professional footing, did not. Lilo was dispatched to Reno, Nevada, for a divorce.[1] In early 1947, Hank and Maggie were married in Henry Schubart Sr.'s living room, a celebration that cemented the father and son's reconciliation over Schubart Sr.'s divorce from Pauline, fifteen years earlier.

It was also at this time that Schubart's desire to have a license to practice architecture came to a head. For too long he had been excluded from opportunities in New York because he lacked a college degree. Unlike New York State, California allowed a skilled draftsman with ten years' experience to obtain a license by passing the state architecture exam. With this professional enticement, Schubart headed west to San Francisco with Maggie, who was by then pregnant with their oldest son, Peter. The move was a critical turning point in his life. As he recalled it in 1995, "I didn't actually decide to devote my life to architecture until I was in my early thirties. When I moved to California in 1947, that's when I applied myself to getting organized and taking the state exam and going to work in an office."[2]

California's licensing standards required proof of study and work, so Schubart wrote to Wright in 1946 asking for a letter attesting to his time at Taliesin. He noted that he had been working steadily in the architecture profession and was applying for a license as a registered architect. He went on: "Although I was much too young at the time to fully appreciate the wealth of material which was available to me, I have always been extremely grateful for the year I spent with you and have considered it valuable experience."[3] Wright must have responded favorably; with the necessary recommendations and a successful exam result in hand, in 1948 Schubart was licensed to practice architecture in California.

It was an exciting, expanding world into which Schubart arrived. In San Francisco, he went to work for Wurster Bernardi & Emmons (WB&E), an important architectural firm whose work was of undisputed significance. Although the firm principal to whom Schubart was closest was Theodore Bernardi, it was William Wurster's philosophy of architecture—and simplicity of design—that Schubart most admired.[4] After World War II, California's population exploded; architecture was flourishing. The architectural precepts developed by Wurster early in his career—the appropriateness of a site for a particular structure, the use of available local materials, an appreciation for the regional climate, and a commonsense approach to design rooted in the client's needs—flowed through the firm's work. WB&E houses featured design elements such as living porches for use in drier California climates; screened verandahs to protect from insects and rain in hotter areas; glazed galleries allowing corridors of light to illuminate interior living spaces; the garden–living room; and the "room with no name," a multipurpose room that bridged rooms having more specific uses. For two decades beginning in the 1940s, the firm's influence was so pervasive that Wurster's simple patio house was a centerpiece of what became known nationally as the Bay Area style.[5] Whether this approach simply reinforced Schubart's earlier architectural views or whether it came as a revelation is unclear. Whatever the case, the firm's attitude toward design seemed to resonate with Schubart's sensibility, and he stayed at WB&E for nearly seven years, taking on increasingly responsible roles.

There was one other important characteristic of Wurster's work that coincided with Schubart's approach to architecture, and that was Wurster's acceptance of any project, no matter how small. It made no difference whether the commission was for a remodeled kitchen or a company's headquarters.[6] Schubart later adopted this same approach in his own practice in California and on Salt Spring Island. In Schubart's remembrances of Wurster and the talented people around him, he expresses the admiration that had been missing from his previous experience of working with large firms: "I worked for Wurster, William Wurster in San Francisco for seven years. Wurster was a very talented designer and had a lot of interesting ideas about buildings and landscape. An awful lot of work he did with Tommy Church, the landscape architect, and they were quite a potent combination. And Larry Halprin worked for Tommy Church and George Rockrise worked with Tommy Church. When I first went to work for Wurster he was Dean at MIT—Dean of Architecture at MIT [and then] left to go to the University of California."[7] He had both found an architect whose work he admired and joined a fraternity of professionals. In addition, Schubart matured during those first years in California. As if to emphasize Schubart's new status, Frank Lloyd Wright briefly reappeared in his life.

Wright arrived in San Francisco in the early 1950s, owing his presence there indirectly to Schubart, who had been approached by the Marin County Board of Supervisors (for whom he had done some work) to design a civic center. Schubart demurred in favor of his early mentor. In his words:

> I said I wasn't interested in it and really not competent to do a project like that. I recommended Mr. Wright and suggested that they meet with him . . . They asked me if I would introduce Mr. Wright at a public meeting in the high school here in San Raphael [sic; San Rafael, California] where the contract was to be signed. At that point, Mr. Wright was famous and everybody came out for the meeting to hear Mr. Wright speak. I stood on the steps outside the auditorium and Mr. Wright drove up in his automobile. He came up the steps with his cape and porkpie hat and I said, "Good evening, Mr. Wright." And he said, "Who are you?" You know, he talked that way. And I said "I'm Hank Schubart." He said "My God, Hank, you've grown up!" Just that way, and we had a jolly talk. I was very pleased and proud to introduce him to the audience that night. He spoke about

architecture and the Civic Center and his contract. It was a very joyous occasion. That's the last time I saw him and the only time I saw him personally after leaving Taliesin.[8]

SCHUBART AND FRIEDMAN

In 1953, Schubart and another junior partner at WB&E, Howard Friedman, decided to form their own firm, Schubart and Friedman, calling themselves "architects and planners." At WB&E, both men had followed the same trajectory upward: from draftsmen to management (as project architects and planners) to junior partners. Although Friedman had a degree in architecture (from the University of California, Berkeley) and Schubart did not, they shared a similar approach to architecture and, it seems, to politics (Friedman was an active member of the American Civil Liberties Union). Their complementary talents made their partnership work. Friedman skillfully used his civic, community, and social contacts to attract clients, while Schubart focused on design quality and overseeing construction. The idealist of the team, Schubart would say "one more design" to Friedman's "we have to produce."[9] And it worked. They carried into their world the lessons they had honed at WB&E, which is to say, they were client focused, drawn to natural materials, and eager to work on projects that were personally satisfying. They also agreed on the need for straightforward design and a particular style of execution: exposed wooden ceilings, wooden walls, deep overhangs, tongue-and-groove plank roofing, and an open, vertical structure. Applied ornament and decoration were anathema to the best modern architects of their generation, and they were no exception.

Their harmonious professional philosophy did not guarantee that they would begin their practice with an abundance of clients. On the contrary, their office accommodations were distinctly meager and their first clients few. Both Friedman and Schubart wanted a small practice with clients who appreciated architectural and professional work from the principals. Early on, they hired a former associate from WB&E, Martin Del Campo, and by the following year, William Sagar, another associate from WB&E, joined them. Schubart and Friedman were committed to limiting the growth of the firm, fully aware

Henry A. Schubart, Jr., *left*, and Howard Friedman, 1960s. Howard Friedman Collection (2000-12), Environmental Design Archives, University of California, Berkeley.

of the effect this goal might have on their financial success. In an article about the allure of a small practice, they described their firm's early days in San Francisco at 52 Vallejo Street, on top of a warehouse for potatoes and onions:

About six years ago, while working together as draftsmen in the same office, we decided the ideas we had in common might make a joint practice worthwhile. Having little cash and no enticing immediate prospects, it took lots of enthusiasm to get us under way. Optimistically, we rented space we couldn't afford, set up a complete booking system, put together eight drafting tables and signed a partnership agreement. Friends furnished some plants, a lunch bag refrigerator and many good wishes.

. . . We decided we'd better take all kinds of jobs as they came along, do them as well as we knew how, and let things take their course for a while. Actually, our first commission was to add a fire escape to a hotel of very questionable fame south of Market (it later burned down), and our second job was a design of a construction shack for a sympathizing contractor.

The first year we did all our own drafting and, except for the tedium of many nights, Saturdays and even Sundays of work, we enjoyed it immensely . . . We decided to concentrate on the less attractive, but more sure meat-and-potatoes of modest jobs. These included some very unaesthetic package deals, some aesthetic houses for enthusiastic young people, a factory that never was built, tract houses, a two-room schoolhouse in a remote corner of the state, and a small apartment house. This first year we each earned about $3,000, a good part of which later turned out to be uncollectible . . . We had more work than we could do, more draftsmen than we had room for and not enough time to really devote ourselves to deliberate and thoughtful consideration of every job that came along . . . We realized that the ultimate results of this continuing pell-mell kind of practice would be a large batch of mediocre buildings (of which there already were plenty), and even though we might make a lot of money, this was not the kind of practice that we wanted. It seemed important . . . to choose the *kind* of practice that we wanted . . . and stick to it. . . . For all this, we work hard and long hours to attempt to make it possible, but we feel *we* do the architecture, good or bad, and that's what we like doing.[10]

Besides offering the informality that appealed to Schubart, the small office provided another virtue: it trained future architects. The partners created preliminary drawings, and the draftsmen drew in the details. Schubart conceded that the most talented sketcher might get stuck pretty consistently doing renderings, but believed that in a small office, that same sketcher would also have the chance to write specifications, detail windows, help with design, and even visit job sites and meet clients. In such a system, he believed, everyone could experience the whole of an architectural practice.

Once the drawings had been completed and accepted by the client, Schubart wanted to be involved in actual construction. He regarded close supervision and oversight by the primary architect as essential and firmly believed that the client hired the principal architect, not the office staff, for this role. Control over the project extended to relationships with builders. Schubart, ever confident in his own talent, wanted builders to execute his plans, not second-guess his designs. His control could be grating on skilled builders and professional colleagues, some of whom regarded him as a know-it-all. But if he ever was concerned that it made him unpopular, he did not show it. It was part of the total control that Schubart prized in a small-firm practice.

Among the firm's early clients was Cyril "Cy" Peletz, a contractor acquaintance of Howard Friedman's, who gave the new firm its second job: designing a small tool structure for his construction firm. More importantly, Peletz was instrumental in connecting them to Sterling Homes, for whom Schubart and Friedman designed suburban tract homes. Their designs were featured in three Bay Area subdivisions for the company: the Rollingwood subdivision, in San Bruno; the Carlmont, in Belmont; and the Montalto, in Montalto. These were small, modest homes with shutters, planters, and functional floor plans, costing around $14,000—an affordable price for a middle-class house at the time.[11]

Another important source of work for Schubart and Friedman was the Catholic Church. Schubart had converted to Catholicism some years earlier, but his firm's success in securing significant projects from the Archdiocese of San Francisco was likely due to an early contractor, John O'Hare, who introduced Schubart and Friedman to church officials. The partners sought a series of projects, and their success on those jobs led to more commissions. The firm was awarded commissions for several significant churches in Northern

ABOVE & BELOW: Dominican University library, exterior and interior, 1960s. © Pirkle Jones Foundation. Courtesy of the Pirkle Jones Foundation and Dominican University.

California, including St. Louis Bertrand, Oakland; Holy Name Parish, San Francisco; St. Vincent de Paul Church, San Francisco; and, St. John the Baptist in Napa. The Dominican Sisters hired Schubart and Friedman for several Marin County projects, including schools, chapel additions, and renovations, and they were the source of two of the most notable institutional projects undertaken by the firm: the library and dining hall at Dominican College (now Dominican University) in San Rafael, California, and the entire campus of the San Domenico School in San Anselmo, California. Schubart handled much of the architecture work for the Dominican Sisters and guided the balance of the firm's Marin County work, while Friedman, who later became a trustee of Dominican College, managed much of the commercial work and many of the San Francisco projects.

DOMINICAN COLLEGE AND SAN DOMENICO SCHOOL

Dominican College, located twelve miles north of the Golden Gate Bridge in quiet San Rafael, California, was founded by the Dominican Sisters in 1890. By the early 1960s, the school was beginning to change from a small college into a university offering a broader curriculum. What Schubart and Friedman encountered when they began work there was a small campus surrounded by large parcels of undeveloped land, also owned by the Dominican Sisters. The firm designed the dining hall in 1958; the library that followed was so extraordinarily conceived that it became a widely celebrated structure.

At the time of the new library project, the school's student population was approaching seven hundred, nearly three times what it had been when the old library was constructed in 1930. After demolition of a nineteenth-century residence hall, construction began in 1961, and the library opened its doors to the college community on April 17, 1963. The Archbishop Alemany Library at Dominican University remains one of the most beautiful college library structures in Northern California.[12]

The library is a two-story design characterized by broad balconies that provide a deep overhang for the extensive exterior windows. An abundance of natural light floods the library interiors through large windows and the emphatic skylights in the main stairwell. The college celebrated the library's opening in its *Alumnae News* in spring 1963, commenting on its beauty and practicality: "It is beautiful in its spaciousness and dignity, in its great vistas from every window. It is practical in the careful arrangement of lobby, reading areas, reference rooms, lighting, and space for moving about without disturbing those who are reading. Its furnishings, which are simple and comfortable, conduce to serious study."[13] In 1964, the Library Building Awards Program of the American Institute of Architects (AIA) awarded the library its prize for architectural excellence, calling it "satisfactory functionally and esthetically and pleasantly different.[14]

While the university buildings were being constructed, the Dominican Sisters offered Schubart and Friedman another project: a new campus for the San Domenico School, located in the Sleepy Hollow area of San Anselmo in western Marin County. With 550 acres on which to design the new school—the scale was unprecedented for the firm—Schubart had an ambitious outlet for his creative vision. His plan preserved trees and featured a stream coursing through the school grounds, with a bridge to emphasize the main entrance.

Dominican University library, interior, 2008. Courtesy of Dominican University.

ABOVE: San Domenico School, 1960s. © Pirkle Jones Foundation. Courtesy of the Pirkle Jones Foundation and the San Domenico School. BELOW: San Domenico School, interior of the multipurpose auditorium, 2008. Courtesy of the San Domenico School.

The sisters had specific ideas about how they wanted to use the buildings, and in Schubart's plans, they found a response to the needs of their mission and the qualities of the site.

Within a thirty-acre graded bowl surrounded by oak trees, Schubart spaced fourteen buildings, including dormitories, a dining hall, a chapel, and a convent for the sisters. He segregated the living areas from activity areas, and connected the buildings with wide covered walkways. "The discussions started in 1962 or 1963. There was a dialogue between Hank and the sisters," recalled Sister Gervaise Valpey, president emerita of the school.[15] "Its setting is refreshing; it invites you out, makes you mindful of what we need to pay attention to and care for." Although the scale of an entire campus was, for Schubart, unusual in its scope, the skillful and direct rendering of functional necessity embraced by the landscape was emerging as a key theme in his designs.

San Domenico School library, 2008. Courtesy of the San Domenico School.

Despite the variety of institutional projects the firm handled, Schubart craved residential work, and his own home provided the site for an experiment. His growing family was by then living on the bay side of the Tiburon Peninsula, in Marin County, and when they moved into their new home, it was unfinished, at least by conventional standards. His intent was to clarify the uses of the rooms even as the family lived in the house—a practice that would be repeated later with the family home on Salt Spring Island. A 1952 *Time* magazine article on do-it-yourself homebuilding featured the Schubarts' home and their ongoing efforts: "In San Francisco's Paradise Cove, Architect Henry Schubart Jr. and his wife are doing even better [through their own homebuilding efforts], and so far have finished $25,000 worth of new house for $12,000 in odd hours over three years."[16]

For the four older boys, there was a sleeping dormitory upstairs, where each child was allotted a bed and a personal storage space. A large kitchen and one bathroom for the entire family were downstairs. The dining room had a table and chairs, the living room a rocking chair and piano. A fireplace dominated the middle of the living room. Hank and Maggie slept on a mattress next to the piano in the living room. In the words of son Dan, the family lived in "splendid squalor," with open stud or plywood walls, concrete floors, and open shelves. The children were prompted to hang a basketball hoop in the living room. To manage the household, the children did weekly chores listed on a "slave sheet." These included cleaning bathrooms, cooking dinner, and making lunches. Cooking with Maggie was a preferred chore, and all the boys followed their father's lead in this respect. Schubart always attributed his love of good food to his teenage years spent in Europe. Whatever the source, he was a good cook, and a Mediterranean diet rich in olive oil and garlic was his lifelong favorite.[17]

It was a bucolic time: Schubart's practice with Friedman was prospering, and his family was healthy and growing. It was into this world that Hank's two daughters from his first marriage reentered his life. Their arrival in California moved them from the fringes of his world to the center and introduced them to his family with Maggie. A house full of teenagers prompted a move back

FACING: Hank Schubart and his five sons in the Marin County hills. © Maggie Schubart. Courtesy of Peter Schubart.

to San Francisco, where a bus pass and a house key could easily substitute for the car travels that were a necessary part of life in Tiburon. Hank and Maggie bought a large Victorian house on the edge of the Pacific Heights neighborhood and soon were invested in the exciting politics of 1960s San Francisco, with its social networks of like-minded, peace-oriented people. Maggie joined the Voices of Women and started a disarmament group. Both Hank and Maggie were active in antiwar protests and civil rights activities.

As his firm's practice moved more toward commercial and institutional work, Schubart claimed several residential projects as his own. In one, a modest commission to design a fence led to a commission for a remarkable home in Pacific Heights, featuring panoramic views north to Alcatraz and west to the Golden Gate Bridge, as well as a moveable skylight. Across San Francisco Bay in Sausalito, the owner of a steeply sloping triangular lot bordered on three sides by neighbors and traffic insisted that the house be limited to 1,200 square feet, compounding the design challenges. Instead of building the house on stilts for easy access, Schubart designed the everyday living accommodations—entrance, cooking, eating, and sleeping—on the upper floor; a lower-level living room and entertainment center were then reachable from the driveway and carport. As a feature article on the house noted: "To plan a house under such conditions, even a mediocre house, is an achievement. But to plan a house that has striking ideas, economy, and personality—a house that takes difficult surroundings and makes an advantage of them—is a success story. As with every success story you find people behind it with unusual talent and energy. Such a man is Henry Schubart, Jr., the architect."[18] Collaborating with Schubart on this project—and with the firm on several others—was the distinguished California landscape architect Lawrence Halprin.

All the while, Schubart remained an active principal in his firm, working with Friedman on most projects, overseeing their Marin County work, and playing an active role in San Francisco's professional community. For its work in the San Francisco area, the Schubart and Friedman firm won a "Home of the Month" award in 1962 from the AIA and the *San Francisco Chronicle*, and received a citation award from the Northern California and East Bay chapters of the AIA in 1963. Well-versed in institutional and residential work, Schubart began shifting his interests from a commercial architecture practice toward larger community interests.[19]

Working with Claude Stoller, an architecture professor at the University of California, Berkeley, Schubart turned his attention to community design, whose goal was to offer San Francisco's poor communities access to architectural services as a redevelopment tool. As established by Stoller, the San Francisco Community Design Center was to host the internship component of a continuing-education program in environmental design, and Schubart became its first director. Launched in January 1967 as one of the first design centers in the country, it was housed in an old university extension building in downtown San Francisco near the Haight-Ashbury district. Schubart, as a longtime top-ranking San Francisco architect, was the obvious choice to be its first executive director, combining, as he did, a passion for socially oriented architecture with a wealth of experience working among the poor.[20]

The Community Design Center was modestly funded by the UC Berkeley Extension and then by the U.S. Department of Health, Education and Welfare's Title I Higher Education Fund. As one of the first design centers in the country, it offered poor communities in the western area of San Francisco the opportunity for large-scale community redesign. Open in the evenings and staffed by architectural graduates working under experienced architects' watchful eyes, it served an advocacy role for community planning and redesign, consequently laying the groundwork for significant contributions to architectural education. Its "advocacy planning" role helped bolster the bargaining position of individuals or communities in challenging governmental decisions regarding urban growth.[21]

The design center's efforts to empower people who would otherwise not have had access to an architect was, for Schubart, the chance to connect his social and political concerns with his professional training. He attended community meetings, publicized the center's staff and work, and worked with local community residents, professors at the University of California, Berkeley, and an advisory board of professionals in order to establish the center's reputation. This work was, for Schubart, an activity that not only augmented his practice, but also came to represent a new model for an alternative practice, one that he would follow in the years to come on Salt Spring Island.

BY 1967, SCHUBART AND FRIEDMAN were moving in different directions. Friedman had a pragmatic acceptance of his clients' political views. For Schubart, if clients shared his social views, shared his politics, had a passion about their home, or were a young couple just starting out, they could receive a disproportionate amount of his time in relation to the amount they could afford to pay. And if Schubart did not like a client's attitudes, he had no problem dismissing him or her.

For fifteen years, Schubart and Friedman had built their Bay Area practice. They designed hospitals, schools, and churches. They designed factories, warehouses, stores, offices, a firehouse, and playgrounds. They designed subdivisions and private residences. In short, they were successful, building an admirable and enviable reputation in the state. (In 1960, Friedman was president of the California Board of Architectural Examiners, and Schubart was the secretary of the Northern California Chapter of the AIA.) But by the end of 1967, the time was right for the partnership to come to a natural, amicable end. They each had bright possibilities in the days ahead. Friedman would go on to teach in the College of Environmental Design at the University of California, Berkeley, eventually becoming chair of the Architecture Department.

And Schubart? He would design houses of a quality that "combined the humanism of Frank Lloyd Wright, the redwood regionalism of the Bay Area style, and profound social integrity in an architecture of rare warmth and civility," upholding "the best principles of modernism as a fine art and a fulfillment of human needs."[22] There are no better words to describe the structure that remains his California residential masterwork—the Pirkle Jones house.

CHAPTER 4

AN EMERGING SENSIBILITY

THE PIRKLE JONES HOUSE

 N 1959, THE OWNERS OF FIVE ACRES in Marin County, California, wanted to create a small development that would look as if the homes had left the pines, oaks, and stately redwoods undisturbed. A visitor to Marin County today sees suburban villages of tiled roofs and stucco castles, but when the artists Pirkle Jones and Ruth-Marion Baruch (Jones) first laid eyes on it, they saw a paradise of shady oaks and evergreens.[1] Introduced to Schubart by the painter Martin Baer (whom Schubart had first met in Paris as a teenager) and Baer's partner, the photographer Nata Piaskowski, the Joneses hired Schubart's firm to develop the property. Offered this opportunity on a parcel of land he regarded "as remote as the Sierras," Schubart claimed the project as his own.[2]

Schubart's first challenge was to devise a master plan for subdividing the rural acreage. Besides being renowned photographers, both owners were conservationists, interested in preserving the woodlands, flowing creek, dense ground cover, and isolation of the extraordinary site. Because they would be living on the property, the Joneses also wanted assurances that future building and land use would preserve a private sense of the natural surroundings. For Schubart, this project offered a rare opportunity to give full rein to his talents: to create a long-term plan for the entire property and to design a home in a rural environment that would reflect his own artistic sensibilities about scale, organic planning, and refined execution.

LAND USE PLANNING

In the years to come, both photographer clients would make their mark by chronicling social and environmental changes to their beloved California. The Joneses asked Schubart to devise strict covenants regarding future development, including density restrictions and architectural standards that would limit what purchasers of the other lots could build.[3] Schubart's planning goal was to balance easy access to roads, sun exposure, and views of the surrounding woods with privacy for each of the subdivided lots. Perhaps most importantly to Schubart, the covenants would ensure that the shared experience of living in proximity to others would not seem intrusive. He reflected on these restrictions in a letter about the house to *Progressive Architecture*: "In some ways, I think the subdivision itself is as meaningful as the house especially since we also developed a set of very strict covenants to run with the land to control design, tree cutting and other important environmental factors. No carport entities are permitted from the main road which therefore keeps its uncluttered and rural quality. The road access to the lots is over an easement which was graded by eye to suit the land."[4]

With the restrictions in place, the Joneses marketed the remaining lots with a portfolio of the site plans and photographs of the surrounding acreage and foliage, in order to limit interest to those who wanted a rural property. Lot B, the largest parcel, was reserved for the Jones home; one other lot was sold. Sales of the remaining two lots would finance construction of the Jones home. The marketing materials stated:

> We, the owners of some of the most beautiful acreage . . . wish to announce that two building sites are available to parties who not only would like to live in this area, but who would also desire to preserve the feeling that it now possesses. This consideration is particularly important to us, as we intend to retain and occupy parcel B as our own residence. We wish each of the four sites to remain in harmony with its natural surroundings, so that when the area is fully developed, it shall, as nearly as possible, be the same natural aesthetic entity it now is.
>
> It is with this in mind, that we not only had architect Henry Schubart, Jr. design a unit plan, so that each building site has privacy, sunshine, and a screen of trees, but that we also provided reasonable protective measures to insure the perpetuation of this plan.[5]

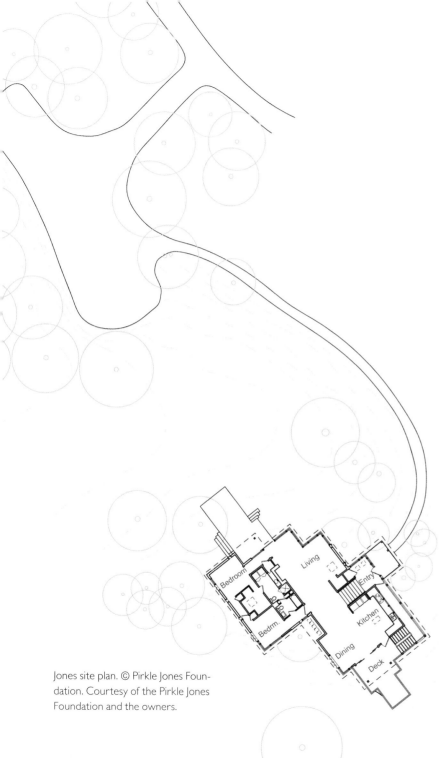

From the beginning, Schubart considered site development, landscaping, and house design to be components of an integrated whole. The Joneses wanted two bedrooms, a darkroom that would be convertible to a future bedroom, an open living room–dining room space, a kitchen, and two bathrooms. They wanted no trees to be cut down, but still wanted an uninterrupted view of Mount Tamalpais. They ignored the suburban convenience of having a garage close to the house, electing instead to keep the carport entirely separate from the house, with a walkway through the woods connecting to the entrance.

From the front of the house to the back porch, the house was designed to rise one story to match the grade of the hillside. Outside the dining-room window, a ledge for window-washing softened the height of the house on its elevated side.

Inside, the interior walls feature specially manufactured unfinished redwood panels, which were selected by Jones while working for the Professional Redwood Association. Rough redwood was also employed on the ceiling. Rough redwood boards and a batten exterior carry the horizontal detail of the eaves from exterior to interior so that the structural and trim details are indistinguishable from outside to inside. Mahogany screeds on the concrete floor and delicately crafted mullions were used to create a house characterized by lightness of mass.[6]

The use of so much redwood meant that the house could be dark. Schubart's design allowed for single-pane glass to usher in light; the redwood finishes play subsidiary roles of quietly connecting the house to the woods beyond. With no visible neighbors, his clients needed no curtains, no window blinds, nothing that would separate them from nature.

By late 1968, one of the four parcels still remained unsold. At the request of Jones, Schubart prepared design sketches illustrating how a house could be built economically and simply on this steep lot. This approach helped sell the lot, and the new owners hired Schubart, by then living on Salt Spring Island, as their architect. Schubart contacted a former Schubart and Friedman architect, Niels Enevoldsen, to manage the construction drawings and supervision. As

Jones site plan. © Pirkle Jones Foundation. Courtesy of the Pirkle Jones Foundation and the owners.

Jones house from the upper road, mid-1960s. © Pirkle Jones Foundation.

would become a habit in his later Salt Spring Island practice, when clients had limited finances, Schubart defined the essential elements of the house, then added features and finishes as budgets expanded. The house, finished in 1969, is a fitting tribute as Schubart's last California project. In the early 1970s, Schubart was approached to design a third house in the subdivision, what he called a "personal trilogy," but it was not to be.[7]

Through the efforts of its owners, the Jones house was featured in *Progressive Architecture* in March 1969. Schubart was not shy about his design talents, but it was not his habit to promote his work in professional journals. The house, wrote Schubart to the magazine's editor, "flows out to the ground on the north and comes out in the treetops on the south at the deck. The long living-dining space bridges this change of 'altitude.'"[8] Accompanied by Jones's remarkable photographs, the article included these comments:

Jones house, sculptural elements visible from inside and out; window-washing ledge extending from the exterior to disguise the hillside grade. © Pirkle Jones Foundation.

Jones house on approach from the carport. © Pirkle Jones Foundation.

Determined as he was to make the Jones house a graceful one in its setting, architect Schubart still did not indulge in any fake rusticity. The masses of the house are prismatic and flat-roofed, the trim detailing neat in a rather Taliesin-esque way. The woodwork, though unpainted, is manifestly machine-cut and nail-assembled. Thin, cornice-like ledges, detailed the same inside and out, pass through the broad window planes to give the house the character of an open pavilion sketched out in vertical and horizontal planes—some broad, some opaque—that intersect.

To keep the house from being overly egregious on the site, Schubart broke up its abstract character in two ways. First of all, he broke up its over-all massing and the rhythms of its parts. He treated the house generally as a cluster of forms, rising to various heights. He varied the rhythms of supporting posts and of mullions, applied (with his own hands) a random-width vertical siding, treated the exterior balustrades and the pergola-like sunshade over a basement window as De Stijl–like or quasi-Japanese compositions of complicated form.

Without making the composition seem disorderly, he thus softened the visual effect. Again, through the same means and through others, he made the onlooker constantly aware that this is a house pieced together with boards, joists, mullions, posts, and scantlings [and] in this way, the abstract composition has been realized in the truest senses—that is, turned into a thing. This is a house manifestly made of wood; even the tan cement floor has mahogany boards, their edges visible, embedded in it. To emphasize the woodenness, Schubart cheated a little: the concrete-block basement is nearly invisible; the chimney is covered with wooden siding. Only the fireplace allows the masonry of the house to appear in any conspicuous way.[9]

Just as important to Schubart as the architecture were the clients: they were talented artists who gave him free rein to come up with designs that would show reverence for the land. In his words, the project offered:

Wonderful, patient and concerned clients, a fine site. The kind of a job that only an architect can do personally and on his own. No draftsmen. Personal supervision during construction. The kind of a job no one can afford to do, loves doing it, and should do regularly if you love architecture.[10]

Jones house, entry hall. A dropped ceiling gives the room human scale.
© Pirkle Jones Foundation.

The Jones house, completed in February 1966, signalled a change in Schubart's appetite for work. No longer satisfied with managing an architecture firm, with its pressures to find and serve clients, he relished his work on the Jones project. In 1967, Schubart undertook a residential project for a couple from Sausalito, California. They wanted a new home in Canada, on Salt Spring Island, and hired Schubart to design a house on a hilly plot of land above a rocky beach overlooking the mouth of Ganges Harbour. The island beckoned him professionally at a moment when he was seeking to work in a community where his creative practice would make a difference. After his first trip to the island, Schubart returned home to San Francisco and announced that he had found the place where they could live. This modest project would usher in the next turning point in his life.

Jones house, interior view of the entry hall and dining area, 2008. The vase on the table was a housewarming gift from the photographer Dorothea Lange.

CHAPTER 5

SALT SPRING ISLAND

 N FALL OF 1967, Hank and Maggie announced that they were moving with the younger children to Canada, and they arrived on Salt Spring Island on March 26 the following year. For many years to come, the family would gather on the anniversary of their arrival to celebrate their new beginning. What the Schubart family found on Salt Spring was a far cry from the active and engaged urban life they had left behind in San Francisco. It was a new country, a new climate, a new community, with one client, no friends, and no home—truly, a leap of faith. There was much to learn and much hope for the future.

BACK TO BASICS

Hank Schubart's arrival on the island was greeted by locals with a collective shrug. In time, the island's population would embrace him, but in 1968, it was slow to welcome new residents. The island architecture that he encountered was compact and pragmatic. People built small houses close to the road and away from the water, without much regard for the beauty of the structure or the site. Trees were cleared from around houses in order to prevent power outages and roof damage from falling limbs. These houses were similar to the New England "little boxes" that Schubart abhorred.

The Schubarts were not the only newcomers; the late 1960s brought many other new arrivals. Retirees and artists, people seeking vacation homes, and young men fleeing the U.S. military draft were all drawn by the island's temperate climate and low real estate prices. Newcomers meant a demand for new, and potentially different, housing.

A local historian described the new arrivals: "Many other newcomers were seeking a change of lifestyle. Some wanted to bring up their children in what they considered a healthier community. Some left lucrative professional jobs, choosing a reduced income, fewer creature comforts, and a simpler life in a beautiful place. Many were willing to try menial, sometimes physically demanding jobs. Newcomers also included artists and craftspeople attracted by a congenial environment of like-minded people."[1]

Once settled, the Schubarts were determined to show that they were there to stay, and found ways to become active in the community. Their school-age children enrolled in the local schools. The youngest Schubart, Gabrielle, was ten when they arrived; Dan Schubart celebrated his eighteenth birthday one month before the family moved to the island. "I finished the last three months of high school on the island. I went from a graduating class of 1,800 in San Francisco to about forty in my class on Salt Spring," he recalled.[2] Daughters across the island reported the news of the Schubart boys' arrival. They were cosmopolitan California boys who had been to war protests.

Hank and Maggie worked hard to overcome perceptions that their move to the island was a flirtation. There was another perception to conquer, too: Americans were often seen as being too pushy. While steadfast in their support for community planning, social justice, and the environmental movement, Hank and Maggie tried to refrain from asserting their views in a way that would make them seem forceful. An artist and musician, Maggie invested her time in social causes, particularly those related to peace and women's issues. Schubart moderated his usual assertive style, but his progressive—even left-leaning—views still came through. How strange it must have seemed to the island residents when Schubart, still an early arrival, proposed that Salt Spring's economy be structured so that no one was paid more than anyone else. In the end, it did not come to much, but he did barter with a tailor to make some shirts for him in exchange for designing her house. Although conflicts about planning and environmental issues were to come, these initial efforts by Hank and Maggie to connect with the local community went a long way toward diffusing any resentment of them as American interlopers.

Another decisive step cemented them to the island. Soon after they arrived, they bought two acres on a promontory point, comprising two adjacent lots, one of which was covered in thyme. Both lots boasted expansive views across the main harbor, and it was on this property that the Schubart family homes would be built. In the summer of 1968, the family's first on the island,

a hot and dry season, they set about clearing the land for a permanent home.
As a distraction from the active social life they had left behind, the boys cleared
the yard of rocks and logs for a garden. Maggie had brought plants from their
San Francisco garden as a precaution in case they had to grow their own food.

The family moved into the existing house on one lot, a "pan-abode" cottage with 700 square feet of interior space.[3] Their first Salt Spring home was
quite a contrast to their spacious residence in San Francisco, and as with their
home in Tiburon, Hank and Maggie slept in the living room, their bed a double
sleeping bag. The coming winter was one of the coldest in the island's history,
with eighteen inches of snow, and the cramped lodgings sped construction
of their new home. The Schubarts also bought a small building on Mulberry
Drive, affectionately called the "shack," where they stored extra possessions.

Maggie and Hank Schubart, just before moving to Salt Spring Island, 1968. © Nata Piaskowski Estate. Courtesy of the Nata Piaskowski Estate and Gretchen Grabow.

Within a few years, the family had moved into their new big house, nicknamed the "Monument," on Old Scott Road and had retrieved belongings left in the shack. A single suitcase was left behind; when opened years later, it contained Hank Schubart's one remaining Brooks Brother suit, covered in mold. This stale reminder from their prior, urban life symbolized their transition to Salt Spring and the simple truth that neither Hank nor Maggie ever looked back.[4]

MAKING A LIVING

With only one client on the island, Schubart feared that it might take time for his architectural practice to provide financial support for the family. He anticipated working as a carpenter in order to supplement the family's income, confident in his ability to navigate all aspects of home construction. He secured architectural licenses in nearby Washington State and in the province of British Columbia through the Architectural Institute of British Columbia (AIBC). Retaining his membership in the AIA, Schubart also joined the Royal Architectural Institute of Canada (RAIC), a national organization that is partly honorary and partly a professional society. Believing that Salt Spring Island offered a promising professional future, Schubart set about establishing himself there. As he put it, "Well, prior to moving here in '68 I went for a meeting with the registration board for the Architectural Institute of British Columbia, otherwise known as AIBC, and discussed my background and my record and brought photographs, plans and other documentary evidence of my training and experience and they granted me a license to practice."[5]

With his local architectural practice slow to build, Schubart traveled as a consulting architect with the Model Cities Program, run by the U.S. Department of Housing and Urban Development.[6] Work for this program took him mostly to Juneau, Alaska, for growth and planning projects similar to his community development efforts in California. In August 1968, he was "still having some difficulty fully adjusting to [the] Salt Spring pace." But by October 1968, he seemed to appreciate the slower island pace, noting, "It's good to be back on Salt Spring. San Francisco is frantic." And within the year, Schubart clearly enjoyed the island warmth and the lifestyle it afforded. As he wrote to a client in early 1969, "I just got back from a six day trip to Juneau, Alaska for a U.S. Government consultation on planning. It made Salt Spring feel like Palm

Springs."[7] Within a year or so of the family's arrival, Schubart wrote to an artist friend who was thinking of immigrating, explaining life in British Columbia at the time:

> We are somewhat remote and enjoying life on our island. Canada is beginning to develop its own fresh culture although it is mostly pretty unsophisticated. Except perhaps radio, TV and the films which are very imaginative and much less commercialized. Architecture is not very good except in a few instances. The Canada Council for the Arts is very supportive but the community as a whole is still in a somewhat impoverished period of pioneering and there is not much money for art. It is much like San Francisco of twenty-five years ago, just beginning to stir.[8]

As he later noted, Schubart set about adapting to the ways of Salt Spring: "It matters not what I do, whether I'm doing a backyard fence or a big house or a large building. My entire operation, since I moved to Canada, has been providing my own personal time and expertise in design ability on an hourly basis."[9] Most of his new clients had never worked with an architect, and nearly all were wary of costs. By charging a reasonable hourly fee, he opened his practice to a variety of projects, which allowed people unfamiliar with architecture to understand the scope of his talents. Most importantly, he found ways to accommodate the budgets of islanders, from those who could afford small sums to the very affluent. Sometimes the job was limited to site selection or to building only to the "lock up" stage in order for clients to save construction-oversight costs. ("Building to lock up" generally involves construction of the main structure, windows, and doors; it does not include things like plumbing, electrical services, cabinets, or painting.) Or sometimes he would reduce his fees—or the scale of the project—particularly if the clients shared his philosophy or politics, as he had done in San Francisco. At the same time that a wealthy client hired him to design an elaborate home in the Bahamas, an island farmer called to ask for advice about a house addition. The farmer said he could not afford to hire him, and Schubart replied, "How do you know?" Schubart looked at the renovation plans and redrew the design. His payment? The grateful farmer offered him a pig. Martin Ogilvie, an island resident, recalled asking Schubart to design a house for him: "I saved a month's salary, which was a little over $550 in 1972, and Hank agreed to design a house. I managed the construction myself, and Hank checked on it on his own time without charging me, and told me what changes to make [as construction progressed]."[10]

For many people, however, professional architectural services were an additional, unnecessary cost. Designs could seem expensive, even to the island's wealthier residents. Nonetheless, those living elsewhere and building a second home or a retirement home on Salt Spring needed someone to manage the project construction locally in order to make sure that the house was built as designed. Schubart relished that role—and the quality control it afforded him. His plans might call for trees to be left close to houses or to shoot through decks, or for walkways to bridge entrances over steep hillsides. The sophistication of his designs required tight control of their execution. Writing to an early client who was surprised at the estimate of the total architectural costs, Schubart explained, softly and persuasively, why his work was both valuable and affordable:

> Next time you come to the island, I will show you a completed preliminary set and a completed set of working drawings so you can see better what further work is involved. Of course, in many cases, houses are built from "house plans" which are the equivalent of our preliminaries (and you may wish to do this) but in my opinion the judgment of most builders as regards detail is poor and the final job looks it. Knowing the problems of building on the island and giving the job adequate supervision I would guess that my total fee would run about $3500. This is a lot of money but I have yet to have a client regret it in the long run. I would be happy to do further work on the house if you feel it appropriate. It is a beautiful site and should prove an exciting job.[11]

Schubart offered quality control to his clients, and control was in his nature. He placed himself squarely between the contractor and the owners, managing each relationship independently. Contractors learned early on that there was a chain of command and that only one person was in charge of the chain. Norm Twa, a well-regarded excavator and a longtime Schubart associate, reflected on Schubart's unforgiving rules for tradesmen and contractors:

Hank had three main rules: you don't get full information on the job; don't be late; and don't miss an appointment. Hank would encourage people to do it his way. If you didn't do what Hank wanted, he wouldn't call you. If you missed an appointment or were late he just wouldn't call you. I think I was fired three times by Hank. He demanded better quality and demanded workmen stick to their quoted prices. I'd always add twenty percent to Hank's bids because there would be more work involved. Hank liked to build a well-built house. His name meant a lot to him.[12]

The island's best builders sought to work with Schubart. His was interesting work focused on quality structures. Confident in his knowledge of construction techniques, Schubart specified what he wanted and watched for builders who paid attention to his specifications. He also carefully checked the work, so the contractors with whom he worked learned to set high standards. If contractors wanted to learn, he would teach them. If they were not interested in learning from Schubart, he was not interested in them.

By the time a contractor was selected, Schubart had interviewed the clients, visited the site, and considered the schedules of contractors with whom he had positive experiences. He managed all billing, payment, quality-control, and design decisions, and woe unto the contractor who tried to go around him to speak directly to the client. A builder who had a question was to ask Schubart. "You're not to talk to my clients," Eddy Jang, an early Schubart contractor, was told. "They were Hank's clients. He was good to his clients. The client was king with Hank."[13] The effect of his standard of excellence was to raise expectations about home-building quality on the island. Contractors and subcontractors began to be proud to be selected for a Schubart job. The homes he was designing did not look or feel like other island houses. Residents took note and would ask of a particular house, "Did an architect do this?"

In the midst of establishing his practice and defining its sensibility, Schubart began designing a large home for his family (the Monument, mentioned earlier), to be located next door to the project—for the Newbecks—that had first drawn him to Salt Spring Island. The preliminary plans for Schubart's first Salt Spring project had been drafted before he left California, but financial concerns played havoc with the project. Finally, in late 1968, construction began on the Newbeck house. The house exterior was constructed from locally milled cedar cut into random-width boards and battens, a pattern that would be repeated over and again in future projects. Shallow overhangs provide modest shade in the summer and protection during long wet winters. Only the large fireplace, integral to the house's design, remained untouched from the preliminary plan. Large glass panes frame southerly views over the island's main harbor, and clerestory windows on the north allow in light without a loss of privacy. Skylights, the first to be seen on the island, offer additional natural light.

Construction on Schubart's own house began in 1970 and was finished in 1971; the entire family did much of the work, with the help of only a few subcontractors. All children were expected to help; daughter Gabrielle, age twelve, picked up scrap lumber and shingles, sanded, and helped stain the cabinets. The Monument, which showcased his architectural skills, was the Schubart home until the 1980s. (In the early 1980s, Schubart built a smaller home next door, nicknamed the Miniment.) Schubart oriented his house toward the south and west, so only by standing on the southeastern deck and looking directly below could someone have a view of the neighbors. Deep overhangs dramatically frame the perimeter; the interior courtyard was filled with thyme.

Newbeck house, exterior front and living room, 2008. This was the project that brought Schubart to Salt Spring Island.

Schubart had a secondary purpose in building a large house: it reflected the family's commitment to the island. Hank and Maggie hosted concerts and other artistic performances in their living room. Since that room had only one chair, other seating was on cushions, window seats, and the lip of the sunken living area, ensuring space for both audience and performers. Any additional furniture would have cluttered the architecture. Flooring was rough-sawn oak that Schubart and his sons sanded thoroughly with steel brushes so that no splinters remained. The effect, never seen before on the island, was smooth, distressed flooring.

One wing contained the living and kitchen areas; wide hallways separated these public rooms from the master suite in the other wing. Two additional bedrooms downstairs accommodated their youngest children as well as visits from adult children.

In time, Salt Spring Island shaped Schubart and Maggie. They adapted to the island's pace and community, while holding fast to their own style. One summer evening, a friend and his wife rowed across the water, landing below the big Schubart house at ten. They pulled their boat up, secured it to a tree at the water's edge, and scrambled up a hundred feet to the house. Crossing the thyme-covered yard, they peered through the large windows surrounding the living and dining areas. What they saw made them stop and stare: Hank and Maggie were eating at the dining room table with ten cooked chickens on the tabletop between them. Invited in to share the expansive meal, Maggie and Hank exclaimed, "Why cook one when you can cook all ten and then have food to eat for the rest of the week?"[14] It was the Schubart rationale. They were unconventional, bringing a bohemian sophistication to their new home.

In many ways, the Monument was a harbinger. Schubart designed mostly single-family residences, averaging an extraordinary output of twenty-five to thirty houses each year.[15] The early houses he designed were simple: two bedrooms, one bathroom, a living room, and a kitchen with a dining area. But they had features, descendants of his California designs, that made them unlike anything else on the island. Broad expanses of glass forged bonds with the surrounding forest, which was echoed in wooden detailing. These houses began the work that he would refine in years to come: skylights and clerestory windows were the most efficient way to bring light into the house; cedar

decks were built around trees; and glass, local stone, and elements other than walls were used to separate rooms. Exposed soffits, rather than seeming un-finished, added to the natural sheltering character of the house. In 1969, a client could have an architecturally designed house—with preliminary con-struction oversight—for $15 an hour, or about $450 in architectural fees, and build it for about $20 a square foot. Schubart believed that everyone building a home needed an architect and that he was the best architect for the island.

From the design and drafting to the delivery of the finished project, from owners to cleanup crew, every person involved knew that Schubart was in charge. Because he was so prolific and because the values he espoused were so clearly delineated, it is little wonder that a shorthand developed to conjure his hands-on involvement. For islanders, his projects had character beyond being just houses. They became "Hank houses."

LEFT: Monument on approach, 2008. ABOVE: Monument, main living room, where the Schubarts hosted musical events during their early days on the island, from 1971 to the mid-1980s. Since there was little furniture, guests were invited to use cushions or to sit on the bench defining the sunken living room.

CHAPTER 6

THE PRACTICE FLOURISHES

HERE WAS MORE TO SCHUBART'S early successes on Salt Spring than being the only architect on the island. He possessed an energetic, confident, commanding presence and consistently sought to persuade potential clients that an architecturally designed house was essential. He could site a house on a large rock bluff or in the woods, obscuring future neighbors and orienting the house to magnificent views. He designed houses around existing trees and contours, teaching that there were alternatives to mowing down mature trees to make room for the house site and then planting seedlings to cover the resulting bare ground.

When Schubart first engaged with clients, he reminded them that their home might be their most important investment. He urged them to invest in houses they could enjoy year-round. Next, he asked that they write down their expectations for their home, a particularly useful exercise because it could highlight a couple's differences of opinion. Finally, he encouraged his clients to purchase the neighboring lot in order to limit encroaching neighbors.

Although he refused to scrimp, Schubart used local materials whenever possible. Cedar and fir were abundant, and the island sawmill readily produced custom siding. Local fieldstone collected from the island's hills, or rock quarried on the island, could be transformed into prominent fireplaces, and materials found along beaches were used occasionally in his houses. In one early house, Schubart used a large piece of driftwood as a mantel.

Schubart was slow to accept new construction technology, such as nail guns and staples, preferring handcrafted construction. Of course, finding skilled building tradesmen and contractors to construct his designs presented its own challenges on Salt Spring Island. As he remarked to one builder: "All this money and effort going into the project and this five minutes you saved doesn't matter. You don't have to go slow but you need to think about it."[1] To an early client, Schubart wrote about the challenges of ensuring quality construction on a small island: "I am continuously distressed at the difficulties in getting things built well and economically on the island. It takes an inordinate amount of time and effort. Drawing the plans is within my control, whereas getting something built involves many uncontrollable factors. The house nearby that was ready to build last October is still mired in mud and ice!"[2]

What Schubart loved most was his own hands-on work. He wanted to be the guy standing beside the backhoe. This was no surprise to those who knew him: for Schubart, excavation was like sculpture; it was art on a grand scale.

BRIDGE TO SALT SPRING: A WEALTHY PATRON

Just before leaving California, Schubart was introduced to Becky Kaiser Drobac, her husband, and family, who hired Schubart to design a house for them on Orcas Island, in the San Juan Islands off the coast of Washington, on Kaiser family property. Shortly after seeing plans for his daughter's house, Edgar Kaiser, Sr., hired Schubart to renovate his own residence in the family compound. Residential projects for the Kaiser family would challenge the architect in the years to come. Kaiser Sr. would become his patron, offering him virtually unlimited budgets and a design latitude that allowed him to create residences about which most people can only dream.

Edgar Kaiser, Sr., was the son of Henry J. Kaiser, a steel and shipbuilding magnate who expanded the family enterprises to include an extensive health care conglomerate. Kaiser Sr. ran the family businesses, and he and his wife, Sue, owned a large acreage on rural Orcas Island and encouraged their adult children to build homes there as part of a family enclave that would foster easy exchange among family members and economize on the sharing of utilities—including a desalination plant. The projects on Orcas led, in turn, to several other Kaiser residential projects, the most elaborate of which was a large home on Eleuthera, in the Bahamas, in 1970.[3] Schubart's palette of native stone, broad wood beams, and glass walls was adjusted for the tropical site and the Kaiser taste for luxurious details. In particular, the project lavished much expense on interior details: French and Spanish tiles on the main living floors, cypress walls in the living room, a cypress-beamed cathedral ceiling in

the master bedroom, marble countertops in the bathrooms, and a one-of-a-kind chandelier by a Parisian artisan. Schubart's usual preoccupation with the outdoors was also on full display. A pergola stretched sixty-one feet to the front door, and glass walls opened wide to the view from the Kaisers' lofty site, one of the highest points on the island.

What a dramatic contrast the Kaiser projects must have presented to Schubart's simpler Salt Spring projects. Because the Kaiser projects were far from the island, Schubart hired local architects to oversee building, and Kaiser company engineers reviewed the technical plans. In Schubart's words: "In all of the work that I did with Kaiser, Sr., the entire building process was vetted by Kaiser engineers . . . and they undertook to do not only the construction, but also all of this other surrounding matter of compliance with codes and local arrangements with building authorities."[4]

In 1972, Schubart began work on a Kaiser project closer to home, in Vancouver. A single ferry crossing or a short floatplane ride from Salt Spring, the home was designed for Edgar Kaiser, Jr., the eldest son. Located on Belmont Avenue, one of Vancouver's most prestigious residential streets, the house was sited below street level with a garden view across English Bay. Hidden from public view were the hand-carved wooden railings and—incredibly—gold-plated pipes for the plumbing. In the 1980s, Schubart began work on a second Kaiser Jr. home, also located on Belmont Avenue. Designed in 1985 and completed in 1988, it contained nearly twenty thousand square feet and was destined to be the last Schubart project for the Kaiser family.

On Christmas Day 1988, just months after Kaiser Jr. moved into the second Belmont Avenue house, a fire engulfed large portions of the house when a Christmas tree caught fire. The tree, nine to ten feet tall and about six feet wide, was covered with more than seven hundred lights. The house suffered extensive damage, and many of its contents were lost. As a consequence, Kaiser Jr. sued the City of Vancouver as well as various contractors, including masonry, plumbing, and electrical contractors; Schubart and his son Michael, who worked on design drafts; the builder; and even the florist who delivered the Christmas trees. It was the only lawsuit in which Schubart was named as a defendant during his long career. The suit dragged on for several years, and in the end, Schubart settled the case rather than endure the litigation. Kaiser

FACING: Schubart on-site during excavation and clearing, 1980s. He seemed to enjoy that process nearly as much as architectural design. Photograph courtesy of Robert Barnard Design, Ltd.

Jr. sold the house and lot, and the new owners hired Schubart as a consulting architect for the rebuilt residence.

By 1988, Sue and Edgar Sr. were both deceased. Schubart had built another house on Orcas for a second daughter and had consulted on potential, though ultimately unbuilt, homes for other Kaiser family members. Schubart also designed a memorial for Sue Kaiser, intended for the family's Orcas acreage. The Kaiser-Schubart relationship, long and productive and, in many ways, a bridge to Schubart's successful practice on Salt Spring, was coming to a close. His work for the family provided him with financial support and opportunities for creativity that were essential during his early days on the island. Despite the hardships of travel, the work gave full vent to his skill and imagination.

In all, Schubart designed or significantly consulted on four residences for Edgar F. Kaiser, Sr., and more than ten projects for Kaiser family members. The work was in California; the Bahamas; Orcas Island, Washington; and Vancouver, British Columbia. But it was the house on Orcas for Becky Kaiser Drobac and her family—the first to pull him into the Kaiser fold—that Schubart relished most. It was, in the words of Edgar Kaiser, Sr., to his daughter, the "house that Hank always wanted to build."[5]

ADVOCATING FOR A COMMUNITY PLAN AND THE ISLANDS TRUST

In 1970, Schubart was Salt Spring's only architect and the only resident with large-scale community-planning experience. This did not mean that the island immediately embraced the accomplished architect's ideas. On the contrary, Salt Spring's developers were wary of him. And rightly so. With minimal governmental rules or standards, island landowners at the time could build virtually anything on their land.

Salt Spring's informal development had resulted in two distinct communities. The southern end tended to be more casual, more "hippie," and more artistic; and while artists lived all over the island, people living on the north end were called the "martini set." But both north and south shared a common belief in little to no governmental interference. This attitude toward uncontrolled land use began to change in the late 1960s with the development of the Magic Lakes subdivision on nearby North Pender Island. Although the

Pender Island population was only 700, this subdivision offered for sale more than 1,200 suburban-scaled quarter-acre lots. Suddenly, residents throughout the Gulf Islands were concerned that their islands might be reduced to small parcels intended for recreational use. In 1969, the provincial government imposed a minimum lot size of ten acres on the Gulf Islands, including Salt Spring, effectively halting development until community plans and zoning regulations could be put in place.

Both the Capital Regional District and the Islands Trust were chartered with preserving and protecting growth in the Gulf Islands. The local chamber of commerce formed the Community Planning Advisory Committee and asked Schubart to contribute. From his experience with community planning in San Francisco, he knew that controlling development was a contentious issue destined to alienate some citizens while pleasing others. Sensing that the essence of Salt Spring could be ruined by its own success, he urged the island to plan for major population growth. Restricted development, he argued, would enable the island to retain its rural charm, and concentrating growth in existing communities or in thoughtfully planned new communities would enable Salt Spring to absorb new residents with minimal disruption to the island's natural beauty. It was a difficult debate, but in the end, people listened to him, even if not all of them liked what he had to say. "He was an effective advocate for his side," recalls Tom Toynbee, an island businessman. "Hank had a powerful following on the island. Lots of people looked to him for guidance on community planning."[6]

Schubart worked with the chamber of commerce to devise a survey, querying residents about future growth. The surprising results showed that a large majority of residents favored planning, zoning, local government, and a building code. The islanders also favored maintaining open and undeveloped areas, hoping that future growth could be concentrated in the three main towns: Ganges, Fulford, and Vesuvius. Equipped with these results, the Capital Regional District adopted the first official community plan in 1974.[7] This successful community achievement emboldened Schubart and marked the beginning of his efforts on a broad range of community projects.

Using the now official Community Plan to guide the island's growth, Schubart undertook commercial projects for both small and larger island

Ganges Firehall, its tower standing guard in downtown Ganges.

organizations. He worked with the local golf club to modestly redesign its clubhouse, and he drew up plans to renovate and repair local churches, the local library, and new commercial areas in downtown Ganges. He designed the renovation of the main fire hall, adding equipment bays, storage and work space, staff facilities, a thirty-five-foot-tall hose tower, and the clock face that still watches over downtown Ganges.

He designed alterations, additions, and new school construction for the Gulf Islands School District, and was retained as the consultant for site planning of the high school on Salt Spring and school buildings on surrounding islands, including early elementary-school designs on Pender and Galiano Islands. With two other Salt Spring residents, Wilf Peck and Ray Hill, he worked to keep school-construction jobs on the island by ensuring that the school board managed the projects itself. This innovative arrangement allowed local builders to participate in the work without having to post expensive performance bonds, preventing the work and its related jobs from going to bigger, more established builders from elsewhere.[8]

Most importantly, as Schubart and his family settled into their home and became established leaders in the community, Schubart began to make his most profound contribution through the design and construction of a series of extraordinary houses. His advocacy for thoughtful growth became a map for the island's future, and the houses he designed became landmarks on that map.

HOUSE TOUR: EARLY HOMES

As was his practice, Schubart began project interviews, asking how his clients lived. "Tell me how you want to live, not what you want in a house" was his refrain. After visiting the site to get a feel for the Orcas Island property, he wrote to the clients, Becky Kaiser (Drobac) and Martin Drobac, in April 1968, remarking on the property: "I immediately had some strong ideas for siting the house. I agree with you that the view up and down the channel should predominate and the general location of the stakes already set out is a good one to start with. I don't feel that the house should be too close to the water edge but by some judicious trimming of trees the view can be kept even if it is set back somewhat. . . . Also, some very careful thought will have to be given to protecting the children from the edge cliff."[9]

His clients wanted a country house that mimicked a barn structure but included all the modern conveniences. It was, in his words, an old barn made new: a twentieth-century house framed like a nineteenth-century barn. The structure was to be of heavy wood posts, the walls of white spruce, all rough sawn, lightly hand-sanded, and waxed smooth but allowing for natural blemishes. Stone from the island was used for the chimneys and for the outside veneer, complementing the light shake roof. On the floors, rough-sawn wide oak planks created the feel of a hayloft floor polished by many years of use. Never a fan of gutters, even in the rainy Pacific Northwest, Schubart regarded them as unnecessary, writing to the owners: "Old barns did not have gutters and rainwater leaders; they did not have weather stripping. And although these details are somewhat inconsequential aesthetically they (and others) will add a finesse I would want to avoid."[10]

Rather than his customary expansive windows to capture views, small-pane windows frame the light. The interior is constructed entirely of wood: oak, spruce, and cedar. Cedar beams running the length of the ceilings in the living areas were gouged with a sharp hoe and sanded. Upstairs are the bedrooms, including two dormitory rooms, one for the girls and one for the boys. Hipped dormers open these dormitories to more light. Suspended from the ceiling beam in each dorm room is a wooden swing tethered by a woven rope.

A rough rock fireplace, large enough to sit in, anchors the living room. Adjoining it is a small loft. Stashed above the upper rung of the loft ladder, a large wooden swing could be freed to swing between the living and dining rooms. Behind the dining room table, a basketball hoop was off-limits only when the table was set. Schubart designed the round dining room table, a large rectangular table in the utility room, and living-room side tables. The dropped railing on the back deck ensured unimpeded views of the water. As the cost projections for this unique structure rose, even Kaiser became concerned. But in the end, the owners wanted every one of Schubart's details. Almost undetected from the water, certainly unseen from the road, the house vouchsafes its handcrafted beauty only to the dwellers.

LEFT: Kaiser-Drobac house. Released from its tether, the wooden swing hangs boldly in the space between the living and kitchen areas. ABOVE: The expansive decks that continue the living space outside have surrounded this large tree for nearly half a century.

FACING: Kaiser-Drobac house, girls' dorm. Since the family included three girls and three boys, Schubart constructed dorm rooms, each with its own swing as a centerpiece.
ABOVE: Kaiser-Drobac house. Rough-hewn beams, given depth by adzing, are used throughout the interior. The main staircase illustrates the all-wood character of the house.

Some clients arrived at Schubart's office through the Architectural Institute of British Columbia, the local professional body. Nancy Keith-Murray asked Schubart to design her Salt Spring retirement house on a hillside lot with an unobstructed view of Ganges Harbour. She wanted to live comfortably as she aged, so Schubart designed the main living areas on the same floor as the bedroom and bathroom and kept the house to a modest 1,200 square feet. That the owner lived independently in the house for twenty-three years offers evidence of the combination of comfort and utility that the house provided. A glass-topped carport flanks the roadside, and an extended walkway serves as a bridge from the main road, creating an accessible, flat path to the front door.

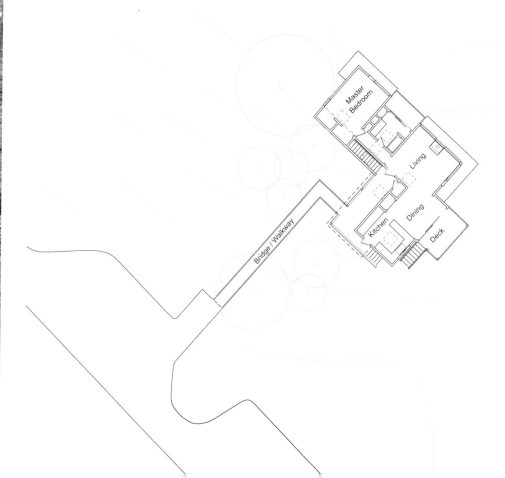

FACING: Keith-Murray house, bridge to the entrance. ABOVE: Keith-Murray house, side-angle view of the window-washing ledge. RIGHT: Keith-Murray site plan.

The south end of Salt Spring offers views from a rocky shore looking across to Swartz Bay on Vancouver Island. Here, the rough elegance of the house he built for Harry and Ilse Leader remains after decades of exposure to the sun, wind, and persistent rain. Schubart initially offered the owners a choice of three sites on which to build. Ilse leader reflected: "He visited the property and then gave us three choices where to site the house: by the water, up on a hill, or in the middle. Like any good Canadian we chose the middle site."[11]

A finished cedar wall partitions the entry from the living room, emphasizing the domestic scale of the interior, while rough cedar beams define the space from above. The flooring is eastern oak, and the double fireplace was built with local fieldstone. This is a rare three-story Schubart house: the children's rooms are downstairs, and the master bedroom and its bath are upstairs. Above the living room is a loft space, now home to a large yellow model airplane. On all three stories, exterior decks extend the interior, emphasizing views to the south and west.

Leader house, living room framed with broad cedar beams, with glimpses of the kitchen beyond.

FACING: Leader house, facing south toward the San Juan Islands. Large overhangs stand guard around all sides of the house, protecting it from the sun's harsh rays.
ABOVE: Leader site plan.

Schubart was hired by Tom Gossett to renovate an existing building in order to provide offices and retail space as well as to add a structure for feed, fertilizer, and storage. The resulting design stands today as a commercial structure with the hallmarks of Schubart's work: random-width cedar siding and skylights in the shingle roof. The heft of the interior supporting beams is emphasized by double posts that combine aesthetics with structural logic. A sliding door declares the robust scale of the barnlike structure. Taken together, the effect is that of a rough but unquestionably elegant functionality.

FACING: Andress house, gabled, with random-width cedar siding and a hipped dormer. A skylight over the master bedroom allows for nighttime stargazing.
ABOVE: Foxglove Farm and Garden Supply. Dramatic in its simplicity, this is the perspective most often sketched by visiting architects. Skylights illuminate the main floor.

Wooldridge barn. An "old hat" farm barn with a gabled roof and Schubart's trademark random-width siding.

As Schubart's practice flourished, the "Hank Houses" became bigger, more expensive, and even luxurious. "He was such a sophisticated presence. So far ahead of everyone on the island in his ability to design things," recalls an early apprentice, Christopher Secor.[12] Having set out to assert himself as a residential architect, Hank Schubart had in effect become Salt Spring Island's "village architect."

CHAPTER 7

VILLAGE ARCHITECT

Y THE EARLY 1980S, Schubart's commanding presence and reputation for excellence were well established. An accomplished architect was good for the island. People felt confident about investing on the island because they trusted that they would have a well-built house. There had been no building restrictions on the island when Schubart arrived, and even after codes were enacted in the 1970s, Schubart regarded building regulations as setting the minimum for design, not the desired standard. While some thought he overbuilt, he designed houses intended to survive earthquakes and last a long time; he had a well-earned reputation as a creator of high-quality buildings. Those who requested the kind of conventional brick houses they had known elsewhere were quickly set straight. In his opinion, "This is the west coast—you build with wood."[1] Although he used brick occasionally, as an accent or in a fireplace, his devotion was to the tall, abundant native cedars.

He had a talent for finding the approach that the client wanted and then melding that with the island's landscape. Approaching every project as though it were his first, and unique in every respect, he enjoyed meeting clients and finding out about their lives. If he liked the new clients, he was friendly. Questions about how clients lived, how they spent their leisure time, or how big a family they wanted would elicit personal responses: clients wanted to have more children; they wanted a music room so that piano practice would be muted; they wanted a separate sleeping place to mitigate a partner's loud snoring. Schubart controlled the initial interviews in ways that turned the process upside down, provoking clients to think about what they wanted rather than whether they were going to hire him. During client interviews, he would use a large roll of tracing paper to sketch concepts. His clients may not have realized that he was applying a well-honed technique.

While Schubart paid close attention to his clients' desires, he alone authored the final design. Clients would say, "I want a house like the one I saw," and Schubart would respond, "You're not them and your site is different." If they wanted small rooms built around their furniture, they were referred to another architect or handed off to a drafting assistant. Sometimes clients arrived with pictures or design books that illustrated what they were seeking. If they started to refer to the pictures, he often refused outright to look at them. He would listen to a client and then go his own way. They won't be getting that, his attitude said, they'll get my house.

His approach was not for everyone. People said they wanted a Schubart house, but they did not always want what he wanted to give them. Several clients hired him simply to site their houses, appreciating his skill at that but unwilling to give him the design and construction control that he demanded. For a client who wanted a two-story house on a lot that Schubart thought was better suited to one story, he remarked, "If you want a two-story home here, you'll need to fire me and get another architect."[2] Occasionally, he himself would fire clients. Why? Because they did not show up. Because they changed their minds. Because he thought they were unreasonable.

And not all elements of every house were successful. A clerestory window with a southerly orientation might allow winter light to enter, but would heat up a room in summer. Or a tight budget might result in a house that was aesthetically bleak. But there was a recognizable approach to his design principles: use carefully observed proportions; use skylights generously; and do nothing simply for decoration.

As Schubart became more established on the island, his manner with clients and contractors became more pronounced. One client, surprised that Schubart's original design called for three pods of living spaces, reworked his drawings into a single structure in order to help him better see—she thought—what she and her husband wanted. At their next meeting with Schubart, she enthusiastically presented it to him and asked what he thought of it. Glancing at her sketch, he replied, "Not much."[3] The projects reflected Schubart's vision. Jeremy Winters, a Schubart client, remembers, "One had a real sense that it wasn't our house; it was his."[4] But Schubart's ownership of the house lasted only through construction. Once a project was completed,

Schubart took no interest in it. Why? The home's essence would almost certainly be compromised by the clients' possessions.

SITE PLANNING: POURING A HOUSE INTO THE LANDSCAPE

Wherever Hank Schubart's gift for knowing where to site a house came from,
no one questioned it. Knowing where to site a house on the land—part intuition, part experience—sometimes did not come right away to him, but
his instinct would always emerge. Usually, clients would arrive at Schubart's
office having selected their favorite spot on the land. "Don't put the house in
the most beautiful place," he would say. If the client disagreed with Schubart's
site choices, he rarely proceeded with the project. He alone handled the site
planning, which established the context for his architectural designs. According to Mark Proctor, one of his longtime contractors: "If there was one thing
he was best at, it was designing the house to suit the site—it was remarkable. I
never saw him blow it. I was watching him one time at a job site, and he came
down the driveway and just sat on a rock for about two hours. Just like any
other artist, they can't tell you how they did it. These were sculptures, and he
wanted to finesse it as it went along."[5]

His methods connected intuition with observation. After an initial client meeting, Schubart would visit the building site with a topographical map
showing existing conditions. This would allow him to determine where to put
the driveway and how to develop the site. He would come and go at different
times of day to see how the light changed and to listen for sounds. Often, he
sat for hours on a client's lot, sketching quickly with markers on a large roll of
tracing paper, drawing circles and outlines. The house would change, allowing
room for trees. He would start with boxy plans and then add angles, which
he called "breaking the spine" of the house. After creating a concept on-site,
Schubart would return to his office and continue drawing, left-handed, on a
flat table with dark, soft pencils. He would trace over the initial drawing and
continue sketching to improve it. Placing the initial drawing aside, he would
repeat the process. Everything was done by hand. And in the end, he gave
his clients what they wanted, even when it was not what they thought they
wanted.[6]

Once he had a client's approval for the preliminary site and floor plan, Schubart was on his way. His next goal was to fit the house into its site with the least amount of disruption, building in and around trees. With the contractor and excavator, Schubart used his antique transit to help refine the siting. Rocks were not impediments to design; he stood on them, looked out at the view, and directed the excavators how to dig, which rocks to move, and which to keep. He tied bits of paper onto trees to be saved and roped off areas that were not to be touched, even if it meant the construction crew would have to work with branches in their faces.

While each Schubart house is unique, all of them display a calculated progression from inside to outside and then to the expanse beyond. After the house was framed, he would walk through it. If questions arose on-site, Schubart would pull his paper and pen out to better define what he wanted. What changed most frequently was window placement. He altered the plans on-site, capturing the best views as he observed the progress of sunlight through the house. According to Richard Dakin, a favored mason: "His houses don't demand attention. Designing houses for Hank was not just for people with money. He drew everything by hand; it was always hand-drawn plans. His houses blend into the landscape. He would just sit and watch and spend hours siting the house. He could see it finished before [you] could envision it. [He felt] that houses had to be part of everything and people were not separate from the houses. You could feel Hank when he worked on a job. Hank was the creator. He was an artist."[7]

He loved trees and was determined to preserve natural places, but Schubart was not a conventional environmentalist. Extensive use of glass meant the house did not conserve energy in winter. Still, the glass had a benefit: it brought in light from every side and allowed views from nearly every angle of the house. Most residences, set at a distance off the road, were hard to detect. If a house was large, he would typically disguise its size, dropping it down into the ground so that its true dimensions were undetectable. A cedar shake roof would further disguise a house in the forest. Robert Barnard, who worked closely with him and then bought Schubart's architectural practice, remarks: "His genius for siting was intuitive. He could produce off the cuff. He was very confident about producing a sketch, and within a very short time he would create designs with freehand sketches. Hank was a sculptor—his houses are like sculpture."[8]

MANAGING BUDGETS

In comparison with newcomers to Salt Spring Island in the 1960s and 1970s, new arrivals in the 1980s were generally more affluent, and they wanted to spend more time entertaining in their homes. There was still a demand for economical homes, but for these wealthier newcomers, Schubart built what he thought the market would bear, while restraining any ostentation. As for the dynamic between Schubart and his clients, Gordon Speed, a favored contractor, says: "These were people used to giving orders, and Hank would tell these clients what to do. They would just defer to Hank, and that these people would just follow his direction was phenomenal."[9]

Schubart prepared construction budgets at the stage of a preliminary plan, and they were often based on early sketches. Armed with these estimates, Schubart might hint at costs and vaguely refer to the overall total. He studied his clients for their reactions to budget estimates, but he almost never stayed within the budget. According to Robert Barnard, Schubart would tell his clients: "There are two ways to design a house. You can tell me what you want and need, and I'll design it, and you'll pay for it, or you can tell me how much money you have to spend, and I will try to integrate your needs and wants into the house."[10] He asked whether clients wanted particular features he favored, asking in a way that suggested that the client truly needed the additions. Often, the final cost was much more than he initially said it would be—if he thought there was room for more in the budget. "You can stretch it [the budget] to the choke point, but you don't want to go past that," Hank would say, meaning that when the client choked on a number, he had found the budget's outer limit.[11] One pair of clients recalls reaching that point: "Schubart would say for another $20,000, we can do this, and for another $20,000, we can do that. Finally, I said, 'This has to stop, Hank. There has to be a limit.' Hank said, 'OK, we've reached the choke point.'"[12]

For clients with fewer financial resources, Schubart might do simple sketches, or he would persuade clients to limit some of the details of a house. He did not want people to think that only the wealthy could afford an architect. He also knew that from smaller projects came bigger projects. As for his perspective on cost management, Schubart reportedly said, "No one ever thanked me for saving them money. But they have thanked me for a beautiful design."[13]

CULTIVATING LOCAL TALENT

During the early 1980s, Salt Spring Island, like the rest of British Columbia, suffered a housing-market decline, but by 1984, the market had picked up, and work accelerated to new levels. The challenge for Schubart became to find ways to manage, even juggle, an increasingly demanding workload.

He shifted from delivering detailed plans and specifications to creating outline specifications, anticipating that changes could—and would—occur in the course of construction. As a house grew, details would emerge. Schubart stayed one step ahead of the contractors and inspectors, building according to general concepts rather than a full set of construction plans. He informally divided his practice into three groups: prospective clients who were "circling," perhaps four to five at any one time; current projects in the sketching stage—maybe three to four; and two to three homes under construction. While he was completing the permit drawings, his construction team would start excavation. If problems arose, he would solve them as they occurred, facilitated by his firm grasp of materials and construction technology. He knew stone and how to work with wood—he knew the inherent capability of the materials.

He enjoyed all aspects of the practice. As he had done in California, Schubart came to rely on drafting assistants, and he cultivated their talents. But he remained firmly in control. When he worked with a drafting apprentice, there would be a dialogue during production of the finished design. Drawing was something he enjoyed and continued to undertake; drafting was how his assistants would formalize the ideas he initially conceived. With client-approved plans in hand, the assistants would draft to completion. Among these were Christopher Secor, now a California architect, who worked with Schubart in the 1970s; and for several years, Schubart worked with three of his sons, Michael, Matthew, and Paul. Michael went on to become a house designer in his own right, and Paul became a designer and an architecture student. Both

Michael and Matthew were well versed in construction techniques. Additionally, Schubart trained the man who would buy his practice, Robert Barnard, who had previously been an accomplished carpenter.

Working with Hank Schubart could be, for assistants, contractors, and clients alike, difficult. For some, it was an occasional challenge; for others, it was a chronic, ultimately untenable, condition. Flexibility and the willingness to let Hank take charge were essential. For all assistants but Barnard, the working arrangement proved satisfactory for a time before an impasse was reached. Schubart had a deeply competitive nature that certainly would have influenced these relationships, particularly with his sons. The key to working with Schubart was to understand that everything went through him and everything had to be done his way. He was not above taking work from other architects, a competitiveness that extended to proposed designs by his sons. If he thought an idea was bad or a design was wrong, he would not proceed, even if the consequence would be to put the relationship at risk.

His clients knew that Schubart liked to work with particular builders and that his chosen contractors had to be hired. Schubart told his clients they would save money by using builders that he had trained, because less architectural supervision would be required. If a builder took a shortcut, Schubart would not use that builder again. His favored contractors knew that the fundamental requirement was to do what Schubart wanted. Schubart molded his contractors, like his drafting assistants and clients, to his way of doing things. "I first met Hank in 1988 on a house renovation project. Hank said to me, 'If you're any good, you'll be busier than you want to be.' I learned quickly that Hank wasn't easily impressed, but there was not a person on the site that Hank wouldn't talk to," recalls Dakin.[14]

Schubart found ways to teach disfavored contractors a lesson. He might reject a truckload of cedar beams, claiming they were not "clear of heart." Or he might require—in writing—the contractor to be on-site no less than 80 percent of the time. If a contractor talked directly to the client, then Schubart would remind him that he did not talk to his subcontractors without the general contractor present, and they were not to talk to his clients without him. If costs increased, Schubart managed the increases with the clients, and if mistakes were made, he required the contractor to absorb the costs of those mistakes, holding the contractor to his bid. In a dispute between a contractor and a client, Schubart always sided with the client. If Schubart could not control a contractor, or if one did not work by his rules, they did not get a chance to work on another of his projects.

Schubart trained a generation of builders to read plans, build his way, and settle for nothing less than top quality. Like him or not, tradesmen and contractors thought highly of Schubart's work. With his builders, Schubart was quick—and confident. "He would never defer to time. You'd ask him a question about a job, and he always had an answer. He would not say, 'Let me think about it,'" recollects Gordon Speed.[15] Schubart paid attention to every detail. He would pull out his thick felt pen and draw on the back of drywall to show how he wanted something done. He was ahead and in charge of every detail.

INFLUENCING A COMMUNITY

For Schubart's first ten years on the island, his involvement with local politics and community planning helped direct the island's growth. In stark contrast with San Francisco, where his efforts were more diffuse, he took great care to be involved in Salt Spring's small community. By the 1980s, his interests had shifted to additional community initiatives, nearly all of which involved a concerned community wrestling with the need for thoughtful development. In his own words: "Well, we live on an island. I have been interested in politics locally on the island because at the scale at which we have lived here on the island, it is quite possible for people to relate on a street by street and neighborhood basis. Or on the basis of their interest in community affairs."[16]

Schubart worked to have urban, rural, and upland watershed zoning ordinances adopted. He helped form Islands Watch, a community-protection organization, and was involved with Bike Path, a cycling organization. He also contributed to the island's volunteer planning committee and its transportation committee. When a debate raged about how to address the sewage needs of the community, Schubart firmly advocated that the treatment plant be built farther away from the main harbor than the business community preferred.

His was not a static view of development: as the island grew, his perspective evolved. He came to believe that strict zoning was too harsh because it tended to concentrate commercial activity in established towns. Self-sufficient neighborhoods would be better, with their smaller commercial centers, because they would reduce dependency on cars. (Both Maggie and Hank were concerned about transportation needs, and from their earliest days on the island, they discussed the need for a vaporetto service between islands.)[17] Schubart was willing to speak out publicly on development issues, and in return, his fellow islanders trusted him. Whether someone agreed with his views or not, all knew that he was on the side of the environmentally conscious. Involved with shaping the community through his building and planning activities, Schubart intertwined his social activism with his architectural orientation. His wife, Maggie, was more active in social justice causes.

In many ways, Salt Spring Island was the right outlet for both of them: Schubart worked on planning and building progress, and Maggie worked on social and cultural progress. Where he was pragmatic, she was passionate; where he was exacting, she was inclusive; where he was impulsive, she was deliberate; and where he was a general on the job site, she was a warrior for social causes. Woven through all these activities was a common thread: they took an interest in each other's affairs and activities.[18] They talked about his jobs and her activities, and together they talked about the different personalities of clients. Still, for the six children their union produced, it was she who wanted to be called "Maggie" and not "Mom" by their children; he responded to "Dad" as often as to "Hank."

They found each other deeply interesting. Maggie reflected on their life together, remembering, "Our life was one long conversation."[19] The renowned Canadian artist Robert Bateman, a Schubart client, was familiar with their activities on the island: "Maggie and Hank were sort of like the boundary for the tide; they fit in and were important. Maggie and Hank were 'it' for a while in terms of activism. They were strong pillars in caring about peace and in the community."[20]

When the Bare Lands Strata Regulations of the Real Estate Act (now the Strata Property Act) of 1976 were adopted in British Columbia, Schubart and Salt Spring Island were presented with a new and formidable planning tool. Created as a way to optimize careful land use, a strata development allows individual owners to separately own their lots and to share joint ownership of the development's common land. In the early 1980s, three large strata developments were started on the island, and with them came another turning point in Schubart's career.[21] The exclusivity of these developments meant that the owners were well to do, and the houses that Schubart designed for them were larger and more elaborate than his earlier ones.

REGINALD HILL

In Reginald Hill, the first bare-strata land development in British Columbia, Schubart was the development planner, as he had been for the Jones development in Marin County decades earlier. This development of 120 acres is above Fulford Harbour, on the island's south end. Schubart designed the sites, lot divisions (twenty-four in all), and building restrictions. He planned the roads, community trails, water and power access, and tree removal. The artist Windsor Utley, who owned the land, turned to Schubart because he wanted to keep much of the land in its natural state. Schubart had a personal involvement in Reginald Hill, buying several lots and designing five houses there.

MARACAIBO

In contrast with Reginald Hill, Schubart did not plan the Maracaibo development; the architect Robert Hassell defined the lot lines, building sites, community trails, and water and power access, and designed several houses in the community.[22] A group of Vancouver business associates and friends had purchased the end of the Athol Peninsula on the island's Long Harbour. Both the master plan and the development guide were created by Hassell and Charles Bazzard, Maracaibo's manager, to protect the tranquility and appearance of the peninsula. Owners were required to design their houses to fit the site's terrain, climate, and vegetation. This was a perfect framework for Schubart's

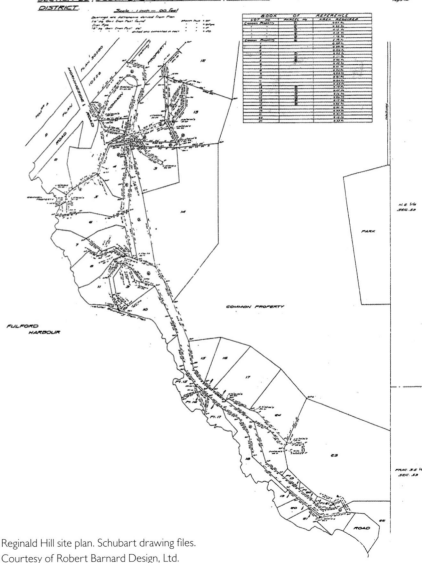

Reginald Hill site plan. Schubart drawing files. Courtesy of Robert Barnard Design, Ltd.

design sensibility: each house had to be tailored to its site, not the site to the 89 house. Of the original fifty-six houses, Schubart had at least a site-planning role in twenty-eight, and he was significantly involved in the design and construction of twenty-two of those houses. More Schubart residences are clustered in Maracaibo than anywhere else on the island.

When the Maracaibo lots were being developed, no one had imagined that so many residents would decide to make their permanent homes there. These were originally second homes for many of his Maracaibo clients, so Schubart often proposed that they first design and build a small structure. Sometimes it was a garage with a floor above; sometimes it was the shell of a house, where they could camp; and, sometimes—if the plot of land was larger than three acres—it was a cabin. For each house, Schubart began by calling for a contour plan of the lot. Some of the lots on the Long Harbour side of the development were smaller but featured spectacular views. Others, on the Trincomali Channel side, were larger and covered by forests. Driveways were shared, and because of the proximity of future neighbors, privacy was a concern. In nearly every instance, he modified the building site that had been defined in the original development plan. Schubart regarded the developer's assumption of where to site a house as a challenge. The developer used circles on the site plan to indicate where houses should be placed. Schubart often thought he knew better, and few who worked with him would disagree.

CHANNEL RIDGE

A third development, Channel Ridge, on the island's north end, was to be a low-density development with a village area, common land, and a wildlife preserve. At 1,400 acres, it was the largest development ever contemplated for Salt Spring Island. The developer hired Schubart in 1984 to manage the development and help obtain the necessary legal and political approvals. By all accounts, Schubart was remarkably effective in securing approval of the development in only one meeting of the Islands Trust, the organization responsible for managing growth and preservation. The anti-development interests on Salt Spring regarded Schubart's involvement as a de facto guarantee of thoughtful development. Schubart also supervised the physical site work needed to market the first twenty-four lots.

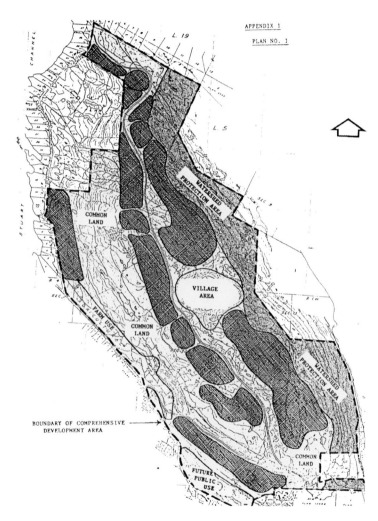

Channel Ridge site plan. Schubart drawing files.
Courtesy of Robert Barnard Design, Ltd.

Channel Ridge, unlike Reginald Hill and the houses in Maracaibo, did not develop in the way Schubart had envisioned. After development began, the developer increased the planned density by reducing lot sizes, straying significantly from the original plan. After this move toward the formation of a more conventional subdivision, Schubart broke away from any association with the development. In spite of this, the developer's promotional materials continued to boast of Schubart's involvement. To emphasize his dissociation, Schubart took the extraordinary step of purchasing a full-page advertisement in the local paper, the *Gulf Islands Driftwood*, on June 27, 1990, reminding the community that the developer should be held to the original commitments. Entitled "A personal message to the community about Channel Ridge," it stated: "Originally I was indeed the designer and planner. However, since early 1987 I have not been associated with the development and have become increasingly concerned with the direction in which it seems to be going. When the ad appeared it seemed necessary to disassociate myself from what was being built, since, in a measure, my personal involvement helped to assure the public approval required." Signed simply "Henry Schubart—Architect," it was a dramatic conclusion to a most ambitious planning engagement.

These developments—Reginald Hill, Channel Ridge, and the houses in Maracaibo—were attempts to create an interdependence of neighbors and shared interests, with public spaces balanced by individual household privacy. For Schubart, these concepts conformed to his view of communities and houses: shared areas for small numbers of people, and houses surrounded by nature, not neighbors. He did not want his houses to shout, "I'm rich!" Instead, he thought the house should say, "I have a level of assets that allows me to contribute to my community." He might have talked about how each of these houses worked, or the register of light in a house. Most of all, he might have used one of his favorite words to describe the houses he was building: "Fabulous."

HOUSE TOUR:
HOUSES FROM
THE 1980S

In the early 1980s, Hank and Maggie decided to build a much smaller home for just the two of them. Construction began in 1983, with Schubart acting as the prime contractor, giving daily instructions to two workers. As with all their houses, he refined the design as work proceeded. They wanted a house no larger than 700 square feet but, after several design revisions, the house was finished in 1986 at 1,000 square feet plus a studio.

Schubart house, portico from the gated entrance to the house. RIGHT: Schubart site plan.

Sun Room

Kitchen / Dining

Dressing

Bedroom

Deck

Schubart house, entrance gate. A stockade fence guards the house from street views and shelters its interior garden from island deer.

A stockade fence erected as a barrier to voracious island deer masks the roadside entrance to the house. Inside, a colonnade with a glass roof structure is supported by cedar columns. The interior courtyard was designed to feature stacked stone beds for vegetables among the apple, plum, quince, and pear trees. From the front garden, only the end of the thirty-four-foot-long rooftop planter is visible. It was planted with squash, whose broad leaves provided shade from the summer sun and receded in the cool months, allowing the fall and winter sun to enter the house below. During construction, an art studio was added off the entrance walkway for Maggie's ceramics work.

The house itself is slab on grade, with reinforced walls, a reinforced foundation, and a density of concrete normally found in commercial construction. Conventionally framed with wood, the house boasts three-quarter-inch birch walls painted to give the illusion of stucco. As they had done in the past, Maggie and Hank experimented with their house. The Schubarts lived simply and did not want much furniture. The Schubart-designed fireplace is a custom fabrication that he carefully controlled, ensuring that the steel was tarnished precisely. The sleeping porch is of crushed aggregate. Wide cedar joists support the ceiling, and are supported in turn by large cedar beams. Sloped glazing forms the entire roof structure, emphasized at the front by wide sliding-glass doors. The porch transforms into an indoor garden in winter.

The back of the house is situated on a cliff, and Schubart stepped the decking down, always conscious of views, perspective, and elevations. The house is a glass box, a piece of furniture framed by nature, undetectable from the road, the air, or the sea. "It was the perfect two-person house for people who really liked each other," observed daughter Gabrielle.[23]

ABOVE: Schubart house, kitchen area, which is three steps below the at-grade sunroom (sleeping porch) entrance. BELOW: Schubart house, hallway. This view takes in the suspended firebox, looking back into the bedroom. Bookshelves segregate the personal sleeping and dressing areas from the hallway.

Helen and Gordon Keys purchased an extraordinary lot with broad views of Ganges, St. Mary's Lake, and the other Gulf Islands. Given the sloping site, Schubart designed a cedar walkway as a bridge to the house's entrance.

The exterior is constructed of Schubart's characteristic random-width cedar siding. Even the garage doors are disguised behind a random-width veneer, which was applied after construction.

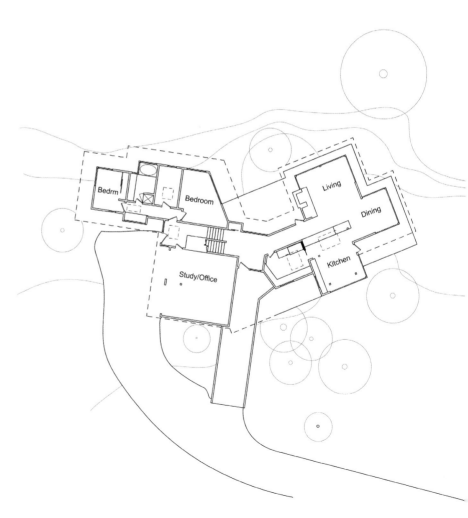

FACING: Keys house, main living area viewed from the side deck. On a clear day, the view extends across the Gulf Islands. ABOVE: Keys house, Schubart's original drawing (Schubart architectural files). RIGHT: Keys site plan.

FACING: Keys house. A bridge of wide cedar planks marks the entrance. ABOVE: Keys house, kitchen. The glazing and framing assembly is supported by cedar joists and large beams.

"I can't think of a house I'd rather do the dishes in," remarks David Anstine, the original owner of the house. With its views of Fulford Harbour, the house draws the visitor through the front door and into the far side of the kitchen. The living room is stepped down on the front of the house; a master bedroom was added in the 1990s. Above the entry is a loft with its own entrance from the road. It is a stacked house, set into a deep hillside flanked by the water.

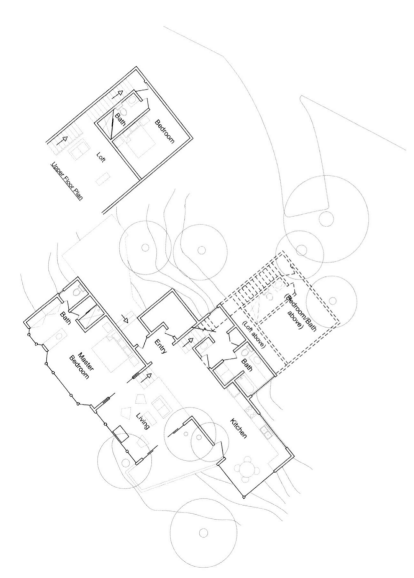

FACING: Anstine house. A boardwalk leads from the parking area to the entrance.
ABOVE: Anstine house, master bedroom. The view is through the main living area to the waterside deck with its prominent tree. LEFT: Anstine site plan.

Anstine house. The well-lighted kitchen opens to the water beyond.

This house was the first in Maracaibo designed by Schubart. Begun in 1981 and finished in 1983, it features two hexagonal volumes connected by functional corridors. It is one of Schubart's meandering houses, and its roofline greets the visitor on arrival from the winding driveway. Once inside, open living and dining areas reveal the harbor beyond.

Overhangs shield the house from the elements, keeping the decks mostly dry. Inside, twelve skylights bring light into the main living room as well as to the stairwell below. A stone fireplace dominates the living room, securely anchoring the house in the hillside.

The architect Heather McKinney renovated the house. She added a library and an art room where the enclosed hot tub and indoor pool had been, but preserved Schubart's floor plan.

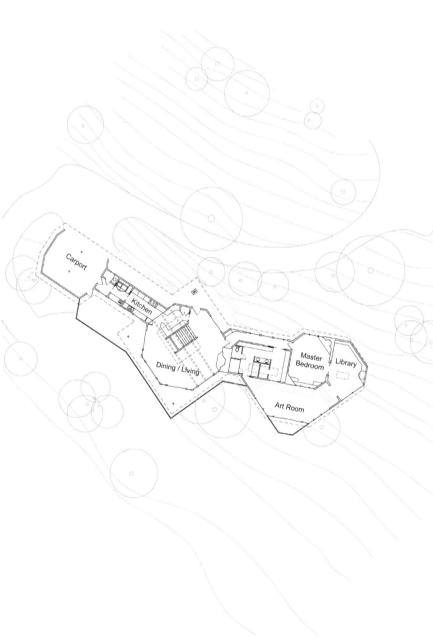

ABOVE: Gold house, library. Working within Schubart's framework, the architect Heather McKinney transformed the original owner's unfinished cedar hot tub room into a library retreat. (See the afterword for more discussion on her work with a Schubart home.) LEFT: Gold site plan.

LEFT: Gold house, on approach. The roofline is the first element to emerge. ABOVE: Gold house, living room. Large cedar beams run the length of the room, supported by four broad cedar posts.

When the owners built the cottage (now the guesthouse) in 1984, they also plotted where the main house would go. (The adjacent Pickering house is profiled in Chapter 8.) The cottage, one of the earliest permanent structures in Maracaibo, inspired several other residents to select Schubart as their architect. The grade of the land dictated something other than a conventional walkway; Schubart designed a bridge, creating both a sense of privacy as well as a connection to the main property. With a living room, kitchen, bedroom, bathroom, and wide decking on its forest side, the cottage seems much larger than its 600 square feet. It features expanses of glass front and back, trimmed by cedar, and is open to the trees.

FACING: Pickering cottage, in its dramatic setting in the woods. ABOVE: Pickering cottage, interior view. Schubart's challenge was to make the 600-square-foot Pickering cottage feel spacious. His design for an open kitchen, dining room, and living room add to the building's volume. BELOW: Pickering cottage. Expansive decks add to the feeling of living volume at the entrance. RIGHT: Pickering cottage site plan.

"People at forty-five build exactly twice the space they will need at sixty-five," Schubart told the owners as he designed the house for their coming years.[24] The lot is steeply sloped, so Schubart stacked the house, covering it with a multiple-planed hipped roof. A trellis marks the entrance through the stockade fence and front cedar decking. There is one bedroom on the main floor, and Schubart located the guest areas downstairs, accessed by a separate exterior covered staircase. For clear views through large windows, Schubart's fabled window-washing ledges were an essential architectural element. The house offers expansive views of Long Harbour from every level and every room.

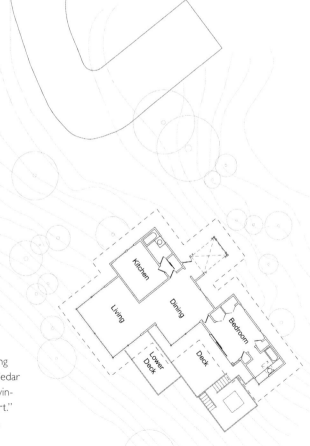

LEFT: Jessiman house, living area with bridge table. Cedar trim frames large pane windows and the "outside art." RIGHT: Jessiman site plan.

Jessiman house, on approach. Vertical strips of cedar siding disguise the exterior staircase to guest areas.

Jessiman house, window-washing ledges.

LEFT: Jessiman house. Exterior ledges serve a secondary purpose for window-washing. Cedar trim frames large pane windows and the "outside art." ABOVE: Jessiman house, outdoor shower. A common Schubart touch. BELOW: Jessiman house, updated kitchen.

ABOVE: Gordon-Sumpton house, entry courtyard, complemented by a cedar fence and a deep overhang. BELOW: Gordon-Sumpton house, stairs inside the entrance, disguised by shelving. FACING: Gordon-Sumpton house, view down to Long Harbour. Deep overhangs protect ledges and the outdoor living area, which overlooks stairs to the water's edge; Gordon-Sumpton site plan.

Built in 1989 (an office addition was created by Schubart in 1995), this house set the tone for Schubart's 1990s work in Maracaibo. The buildable area was next to the road, so he designed an entry courtyard with its own bench to shield the home, surrounded by a capped stockade fence for privacy.

The house is large, although its scale remains undetectable from the exterior. A contemporary lunette window adds additional light; cedar window seats enframe recessed windows. The house is built on a steep grade above the adjacent landscaped lawn.

A few other homes from the 1980s merit attention. Some of these are small, modest houses, notable for their site and their distinctive Schubart traits. Others, standing in direct contrast to modesty, offer bridges to his more elaborate work of the 1990s.

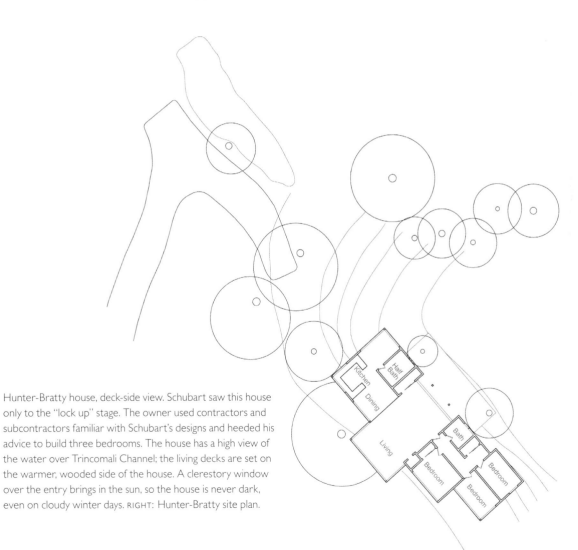

Hunter-Bratty house, deck-side view. Schubart saw this house only to the "lock up" stage. The owner used contractors and subcontractors familiar with Schubart's designs and heeded his advice to build three bedrooms. The house has a high view of the water over Trincomali Channel; the living decks are set on the warmer, wooded side of the house. A clerestory window over the entry brings in the sun, so the house is never dark, even on cloudy winter days. RIGHT: Hunter-Bratty site plan.

Margolin house, living room. A large river-rock fireplace offsets the steel beams defining the space.

THE 1980S ENDED WITH THE pronounced recognition that Schubart's work was, for him, a personal expression. These were not Egypt's pyramids or St. Peter's Basilica. "Hank Houses" were functional homes that used local materials and were sited in ways that respect nature. Anyone seeking a West Coast–style house on Salt Spring Island knew that Schubart was the architect of choice. As more people moved to the island, many decided that what they wanted was a Schubart home. Each feature he included was an attempt to answer the question of how to integrate each element with the design concept of the whole house.

As Schubart began the last decade of his life, he was as busy as he had ever been. Although he had health problems, he often worked seven days a week. His builders needed him Monday through Friday, and his clients would visit on the weekends. His work was his hobby, and his practice was now dominated by work on the island. Steeped in California's modernist tradition, he was forging an emerging Gulf Islands style with his "Hank Houses."

Margolin house, front and deck outside the kitchen. In 1980, the actor Stuart Margolin and his family wanted a contemporary design for their house near the springs for which the island is named. A circular staircase and a glass curtain rising eighteen feet at the front of the house are just two features that signal its difference from many of Schubart's other designs. The house has no overhangs because Schubart believed they would conflict with the glass walls.

ABOVE: Edwards house. Deep overhangs cut in a sawtooth pattern jut over expansive cedar decking. Planter boxes mirror the roof pattern. BELOW: Edwards house, living room, its angles defined by cedar trim. FACING: Bateman Tortoise Island house. A short boat ride from Fulford Harbour, the house is reminiscent of a Japanese teahouse on its rocky perch. The structure opens up as a patio-door module. A gravity-fed water tower supplies the outhouse.

Winter house. A rain chain adds architectural interest as well as functionality. RIGHT: The hipped roof, window-washing ledge, cedar framing, and aggregate concrete with cedar screeds are all hallmarks of a Schubart house.

MASTERY AT WORK

B Y THE TIME HE DIED, Henry A. Schubart, Jr., had designed more than 230 residential projects on Salt Spring Island. In any well-populated urban area, this would be a feat worth celebrating. Occurring as it did on an island covering 120 square miles, it guaranteed his influence would endure.

When Schubart arrived with his family in 1968, it was the right time not only for him but also for the island. The majority of his projects benefited island residents, who numbered about two thousand when he arrived and more than ten thousand by the time he died. Not only did he design residences, he designed civic and institutional projects: schools, the library, veterinary clinics, firehalls, and several churches. He also designed twenty-two commercial projects on Salt Spring. Of his residential work, more than 150 are considered significant, having been completed under his supervision, and another seventy represent design consultations. He brought a depth of experience and perspective to the small island community. With his artistic vision, he created the expression of a lifestyle that was more than simply utilitarian.

Time has been kind to Schubart's houses. They remain fresh and contemporary today, in part because of how he used light to animate spaces. Light enters through skylights and clerestory windows, through large-pane windows, and under deep eaves. Some houses show their age; for example, years of leaves and debris dropping on decks and railings have rotted the wood in some.

Most new owners find that their Schubart houses need an update, but not much more. Unlike so many of his architectural contemporaries, who saw institutional work as a preferred path, residential work was most satisfying to Schubart. "I found," he said, "that the things I enjoyed working on the most, were a few people's houses, where I had a direct relationship with the clients."[1]

Over time, his houses came to be considered uniquely Gulf Island homes—
not Bay Area homes, not Prairie-style homes, not Northwest homes, and not
exclusively modernist. Taking lessons from his mentors, he created a vocabulary of his own. Although reminiscent of the work of Frank Lloyd Wright to
some, his houses were influenced just as dramatically by his time in California
and the sensibility of his colleagues there. In California, he interacted with
important mid-twentieth-century architects, including Charles Eames, Pietro
Belushi, and Harwell Hamilton Harris. Mid-century California exploded with
fine architectural design, and Schubart's involvement with Wurster Bernardi &
Emmons placed him squarely in that important moment. He also collaborated
on several residential projects with the landscape architect Lawrence Halprin,
whose naturalistic approach to design was legendary.

THE MATURE MASTER

From all his early influences, Schubart distilled a design palette for his houses.
He respected nature, building a house to fit the site, even if it meant notching
the roof or building decks around trees. He undertook projects both large
and small, and insisted on the fine execution of his designs. His technique
extended to every feature of his structures. Roofs were a prominent element
in Schubart's design, and they rarely strayed from a hip-and-valley profile. Ide-
ally, deep overhangs would protect a house from the high summer sun while
allowing sunlight to enter in the winter. Roof overhangs came to a fine edge at
the front. If a client insisted on gutters, he would include them in the design,
sometimes setting them away from the roof in order to add architectural
interest. More often, he used a rain chain to guide the water off the roof.[2]

Decks were prominent on the private sides of houses. Always conscious
of views, perspectives, and elevations, Schubart would typically lower the
outer deck railing so that it was invisible to the eye. Or he would design cedar
railing with a glass center so that it framed the outdoor view. If he could not
find light fixtures to his liking, he built them for his clients. Glass and cedar
posts, or glass and steel, created covered walkways that became light-dappled
as leaves and remnants of rain tinted the glass.

Mouat house, a pronounced notch in the roofline.

ABOVE: Variations on exterior lights at the Harris house, Kaiser-Drobac house, Keith-Murray house, and Pred house. BELOW: Southend house, deck railing, in a style used consistently in Schubart houses. RIGHT: Bateman house, covered walkway. Designs for walkway posts generally called for steel, cedar, or hardwood; the cap was almost always glass.

Privacy was paramount to his clients. Even if a house was set away from neighbors, Schubart added fences to emphasize property boundaries. Sometimes they served as gateways to front gardens, while at other times they oriented views toward protected living spaces. An entrance would occasionally be covered for protection. If the back of a house was elevated, he added window-washing ledges—shallow cedar walkways—that reduced the apparent height of the house. Garages were rare: not wanting parking to dominate, he preferred carports, which could be made elegant with tiered glass over a cedar or steel frame.

The exteriors of his houses were impressive, and their distinctive features continued inside. Schubart employed precise geometric designs, often staggering the ceiling height from room to room, to define rooms without using walls and thereby to move light more effectively through a house. He often added a shelf along the perimeter of a room, occasionally with lights inset for additional indirect lighting. Uli Temmel, the island's building inspector, reflected on Schubart's designs:

> The ceilings in many houses were the element that drew the eye. In some, for example, the outward thrust of gently sloping hip roofs was retained by the tops of exterior walls and interior beams under tension, suspending the sloped ceilings without obvious support. It was a structurally simple thing, but gave a very open, light feeling to the space, with rooms and areas defined and articulated by the ceiling structure rather than by physical barriers to the movement of people in the space. It said, "I'm a kind of masterpiece—subtle, simple, well done, elegant; not shouting, not ostentatious."[3]

From his most economical to his most lavish designs, the houses included characteristic features, such as a distinctive off-white Gyproc (a brand of drywall) and cedar trim. He liked wood and loved cedar, and it was abundant in British Columbia. He also appreciated the appeal of the unrefined: exposed beams, unfinished cabinets, rusticated stonework that looked as if a mason had invested little time in setting it, and rough-hewn floors. Even if the trim was painted, he designed the header trim to overhang the side trim and specified that it be crafted without miters. Light fixtures were recessed.

ABOVE: Dymond house, stockade fence defining the entrance.
BELOW: Coleman house, carport.

Master bedrooms and bathrooms were nearly always on the same floor as the kitchen and main living areas, particularly if his clients were building for retirement. Guest areas were nearly always downstairs. Frequently used stairs were set with a long run and a low rise for the clients' comfort. He loved big fireplaces with big flues. Still, he encouraged clients, especially if they were year-round residents on Salt Spring, to install wood-burning stoves as efficient heat sources.

As time went on, he preferred larger windows that would allow for even more dramatic views, even in bathrooms. Schubart designed rooms so that glass was joined in corners, sometimes set back with a post in front to create

In the Winter house, privacy was preserved even if curtains were omitted from the large cedar-trimmed windows in bedrooms.

FACING: A repeated bathroom pattern, large-pane windows abutting a tub flush to the wall and oriented for privacy, as seen at the Winter house. ABOVE: In the Northend house, privacy was preserved even if curtains were omitted from the large cedar-trimmed windows in bedrooms. BELOW: Even a tub at grade would be situated for seclusion, as at the Pickering house.

a recessed window seat. Or he set glass to glass with silicone. If the windows opened, he specified cedar screens opening inward. Taken together, these formal preferences meant that there were few walls for clients' art collections. With all that glass, he knew what clients were going to see if they looked out their windows; if they hung a painting, he did not know what they might see. Art, along with furniture, spoiled architecture for Schubart. "The art is outside!" he might have exclaimed. The art was inside, too, as the houses stood alone without decoration.

DOMINATING INFLUENCE

There was always a price to be paid for working with Schubart. Not every client wanted to live in a house shaped so clearly by the designer's vision. Some clients never returned after an initial appointment. Others, he fired. For contractors, it was strict adherence to Schubart's vision or no more work. He made sure he got his way in any difference of opinion about the design. To persuade clients, he explained how much trouble or expense it would be to build something he thought inappropriate for the house. If a client wanted two guest bathrooms to accompany two guest bedrooms, Schubart would say, "No, you want the guests to leave." If they wanted to be able to seat ten to twelve dinner guests at a time, Schubart would ask, "Why have that many people over for dinner?" If the client wanted beam ceilings, he would answer, "No. In the winter it will be dark, and the beams will make it darker." If the client wanted glass all along the front of the house in order to capitalize on a water view, Schubart would say, "You need to break it up and design a wall to separate the glass."[4] "He could be a bit of a prima donna. He was good at getting a lot of input before pen was put to paper, but once the pen went to paper, it was his vision," recalls John Pickering, a longtime client.[5]

In the end, each client got the house that Schubart wanted to build. "When architects are younger, they have to do what the client wants. There are limits. When they are older and their reputation is established, clients are more likely to give them free rein, and they do what they want. Hank did what he wanted," reflected son Michael.[6]

The 1990s began for Schubart with a cooperative and appreciative client, a challenging plot of land, and a virtually unlimited budget. The chance to give full rein to his imagination was irresistible, even if the project required frequent travel to Orcas Island for his clients, the Godfreys. But Schubart had begun to experience health problems, including circulatory disease. For years, he had smoked unfiltered Camel cigarettes.

Two other events compounded the stress that ultimately changed how Schubart managed his practice. The first was the lawsuit over the 1988 Christmas Day fire in Edgar Kaiser, Jr.'s second Belmont Avenue home in Vancouver. The suit highlighted Schubart's lack of liability insurance, which he refused to purchase, and cost him nearly $135,000 in legal fees and expenses. The second event was a problem with using radiant heat in ceilings rather than floors. Although the use of radiant heating systems in ceilings had been approved by the Canadian consumer safety organization, in 1992 the provincial government sent notices to owners of these systems, alerting them that the systems were unsafe and threatening to void their home owners' insurance if the systems were not shut down. When the radiant-heating manufacturers went out of business, architects and builders were left to design alternative heating systems. The Kaiser Jr. fire and the radiant-heating failures took a toll. They were unsettling events in a career otherwise marked by certitude.

Despite his health challenges, Schubart remained active. He had built a tremendous reputation on the island. More and more people wanted a "Schubart," and while he was going back and forth to Orcas, his Salt Spring clients still grew in number. To manage his heavy workload, Schubart increasingly turned to his drafting apprentices, particularly Robert Barnard, to help keep pace with the work. Barnard's initial connection with Schubart was as a carpenter and a construction foreman, and then as a drafting assistant. Schubart still sketched as he met with clients or visited building sites, but he began to delegate much of the day-to-day work to Barnard.

As the 1990s progressed and work continued to increase, Schubart's youngest son, Paul, joined his father. They worked from Schubart's office up the hill from his house, nicknamed by son Matthew as "H Quarry" or "Hank's

Dymond house, dining room. Schubart believed that the "art is outside," so he left owners nowhere to display any art but nature's own.

Quarry," because it was the source of stone for the Schubart family houses he built across the street. Schubart also had his group of well-trained contractors and skilled tradesmen, all of whom he now trusted to work more independently. These contractors, especially Gordon Speed and Mark Proctor, understood and were comfortable with Schubart's high standards of construction—and the rules of client management—that Schubart demanded. Schubart kept them busy, and in return, they dedicated nearly all their practice to his projects.

Schubart's final career turning point came in 1994. That year, he had heart-bypass and valve-replacement surgery. It was also the year Maggie broke her hip. Until then, Schubart's architecture practice had been all-consuming. "Hank was in the position where he could do what he wanted toward the end of his life. Maggie always thought Hank would quit working. We knew he wouldn't quit work," remembered Norm Twa.[7] The Schubarts' physical conditions were a clear sign that he had to change his seven-day-a-week work routine. He had survived one heart attack and knew that he was not well. He could still scramble up rocks at a building site, but he now held his chest after reaching the top.

In 1995, Schubart made the difficult decision to sell his practice, notifying clients that he would become a consulting architect to Robert Barnard Design. Schubart still engaged with clients and defined site plans and concepts for the houses, but he no longer went in early and stayed late. If a project was challenging or if he particularly enjoyed the clients, he would be more involved. But he began to find ways to carve out more time for himself, and he spent more time sailing. Some years before, he had acquired a sailboat, the *Ardent*. A "Block Island cowhorn," the boat had been built with local wood carved by a chainsaw and hand tools. It was an inshore workboat designed to be sailed by two people, and had gut rigging lined with leather. After Maggie broke her hip, Schubart began sailing with a young man who became his close friend, Patrick Normal. They would sail once a week, with Schubart teaching Patrick how to handle the boat, and as they floated for hours at a time, they talked. "Hank didn't dwell on the past and preferred what was going on now. Despite his deteriorating body, he liked the sensibility of so many decades of living. He was fully engaged, and that gave him a sense of vitality," said Normal.[8]

Hank and Maggie were now well settled into their smaller home, and in the studio there, he had finally built a kiln for Maggie's pottery work. The chimney on the kiln caused problems, and he struggled to make it fire correctly, finally building it two feet higher. On Sunday, February 8, 1998, Maggie had ceramic pieces ready to be fired in the kiln. Seeing smoke coming out of the chimney, Schubart brought over a chair and a wet blanket. He was covering the wood next to the kiln with the blanket when he had a heart attack, fell off the chair, and died. He was eighty-one years old.

Schubart did not like the formality of a funeral and did not want a memorial service. The family scattered some of his ashes in his beloved garden, and his daughters Gabrielle and Mallory sailed on his boat with Patrick Normal to scatter the rest in the harbor. His contractors were uncertain how to proceed without him. For many, he had made their careers and kept them busy. When he died, they thought that was it for them. As for his houses being a tribute to him, he would have resisted that sentiment. His daughter Mallory reflected: "He wanted his houses to be lived in, not be a memorial to him."[9]

Many who now build houses on the island insist on repeating styles they left behind. Tastes change from generation to generation, and as Schubart houses pass into the hands of second and third owners, alterations are made. Still, real estate agents keep his reputation vibrant. "Schubart House for Sale" is often announced in the real estate pages, advertised to denote something special. As the island continues to change, Schubart houses endure. He raised the bar for building standards on the island, and his houses are reminders that quality matters in small communities and in modest—as well as grand—homes.

HOUSE TOUR:
HOUSES FROM
THE 1990S

Godfrey house, living room, which is easily heated by the custom firebox at its center. FACING: Godfrey site plan.

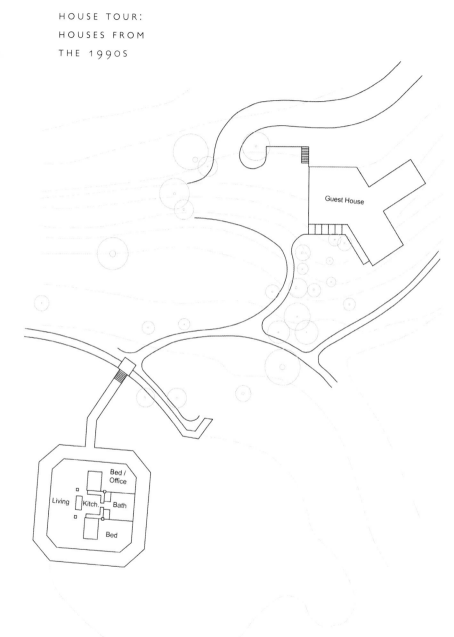

Guest House

Bed /
Office

Living   Kitch.   Bath

Bed

When deciding to build on Orcas Island, the Godfreys were drawn to Schubart's sense of proportion, structural quality, and design simplicity, which they first saw in the Kaiser-Drobac house. Schubart originally planned to build a long skinny house above the location of the existing 1950s home. Traffic noise from neighboring roads made him reconsider that plan. Instead, he built in an ancient marsh, a pond with depth reaching fourteen feet. The entrance is marked by a colonnade constructed of cedar posts. A cedar-plank board-walk, with wide board handrails, bridges the entrance across the lagoon. In the middle of the pond, Schubart designed an octagonal house, like a carousel. The roof overhangs slope downward on all sides of the house, extending eight feet and complementing the open decking at the base. Lacking dedicated support posts, the overhangs declare themselves as a structural feat.

For the landscape, Schubart and Godfrey selected rocks, planted trees, and reshaped the ten acres, especially the parts around the house and down to the water. "It was a poor man's Capability Brown landscape. It improved every year—it looked like it just grew out of the water, out of the land," said Godfrey.[10]

For all its heft, this is a one-bedroom house with a study. Inside, the house resembles a temple, with rugs hiding the pattern on the maple floors. The articulation of the ceiling is pronounced: horizontal planks of varying widths are spaced among joists of oversized timber. Trusses connected by intricate joinery create an apparently random pattern on the ceiling. Spruce walls are set together in a tongue-and-groove pattern thick enough to support the pocket doors that offer cover to the double-frame windows, which, in turn, open to the outside decking. Four pockets cover each opening with the owner's choice of glass, insect screen, shoji screen, or solid cedar. Quarter windows open at the bottom, allowing a breeze to enter low across the floor. Virtually everything in the house was custom designed, including the light fixtures. The firebox of steel and glass, made in Hong Kong, is suspended above the floor.

ABOVE: Godfrey house, under-surface of the overhangs, which extend eight feet. BELOW: Godfrey house, entrance gate and bridge. RIGHT: Godfrey house, exterior on approach; the house and its lagoon.

Godfrey house, interior ceiling of exposed rafters and trusses.

The Harris house was built on a rock ridge in the hills overlooking Ganges Harbour. An exposed-aggregate terrace marks the entrance and continues into the house's entry. Inside, waxed, rough-sawn oak floors are set off by dramatically angled rooms. The adjoining deck is pierced by trees, leaving the impression that the forest is accommodating the deck, not the other way around. Deep sawtooth overhangs add drama as well as provide shade.

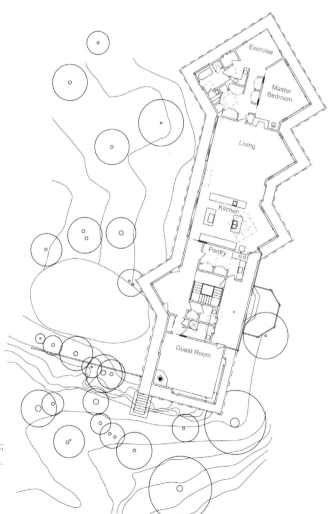

Harris house,
kitchen skylight;
Harris site plan.

Harris house, kitchen. Schubart hallmarks include the dropped ceiling, beams rather than walls used to define areas, and an abundance of cedar.

Harris house, rear deck pierced by a madrone tree.

When the Pickerings built their cottage in 1984, they planned for the eventual addition of a larger house that would harmonize with it. A walkway along the edge of the woods creates the entrance to the main house. Outside, three decks frame the house, two on the sunny side facing away from the water, and a smaller one on the cooler, channel side. Double cedar beams are suspended from the ceiling on short cedar posts, defining the living room. A wide single-pane window is recessed behind a cedar post, creating a low window seat. Since the house has views of Trincomali Channel, the owners left the windows bare, a result very much to Schubart's liking. The master bedroom and sitting area are in one wing; the guest areas and a second study are opposite. In between, the public spaces are defined by a shelf running around the perimeter of the room, trimmed in cedar, and featuring emphatic upward lighting.

Pickering house, the largest of the decks, overlooking a meadow; Pickering site plan.

Pickering house, glass-walled foyer opening onto an inset courtyard.

By the time Schubart began work on the Williams house, he was seventy-seven years old. Still able to scramble over rocks, he set out to determine the best location for the structure. The developer's designated building site was set back; Schubart moved the location closer to the water and oriented the house for 270-degree views along Long Harbour.

Schubart dictated that the fireplace was to be made of river rock and that the living-room cabinets would be of old-growth fir, to match the fir ceiling. The owner wanted a glass wall in the kitchen, and Schubart acquiesced. Abundant light fills the kitchen: single glass panes abut a cedar-trim post to form the support for a four-pane skylight. When the owners expressed concern that the house was bigger than they had intended, Schubart replied, "You don't want it looking like a cabin."[11]

The master bedroom, set on the west side of the house, opens onto a generous deck. Underneath the master bed is a thick rope, which is used to pull the bed onto the outdoor deck for summertime sleeping. The deck railing is four feet eight inches high, set at that height so as not to interfere with the view.

ABOVE: Williams house, deck. Outrigger cedar posts topped with glass protect the outdoor eating area off the kitchen. LEFT: Williams site plan.

FACING: Williams house, living room trimmed in fir, with the entrance totem pole just visible in the foyer. ABOVE: Williams house, master bedroom and deck. A large rope under the bed and double-fold doors allow for outside sleeping in summer.

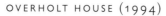

The entrance to this house begins at the garden entrance, its walkway shielded by deep overhangs. Inside, the ceiling disguises the free-floating roof; there is no independent support. Anchoring the living room, with its expanse of windows looking over Long Harbour, is the rock fireplace, constructed of stone from the site. The floors are of wide-plank Douglas fir.

In the kitchen, even the pulls and the bullnose finish for the counters were designed by Schubart. Guest areas are downstairs, along with the owners' second living area, a room that Schubart persuaded them to adopt as a $500 addition. "It cost a lot more than that," remembered Linda Overholt.[12] On the view deck over the water, Schubart added steps to the edge of the deck in order to drop the railing below sight level.

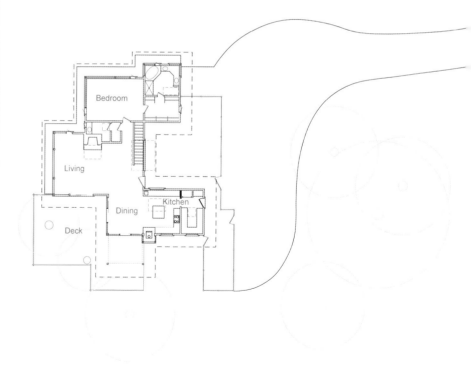

FACING: Overholt house, a gated garden defining the entrance. ABOVE: Overholt house, a fireplace and skylight dominating the living room. RIGHT: Overholt site plan.

Overholt house, kitchen. Schubart designed the countertops and the cabinet pulls.

Beckmann house, hallway serving as a library, with low bookshelves lining the way. Schubart designed the main house and the adjacent cottage; he died before the projects were completed.

There are many more Schubart houses on Salt Spring Island that deserve attention. Among those done in his last years, a few are singled out to end the story. No matter how refined, these houses illustrate the essential qualities of his work: generous windows to invite in light, a structure open to nature, personal control of every detail, and thoughtful site planning to capitalize on a specific terrain.

Hank Schubart's effect on Salt Spring Island cannot be fully described in one volume, and this book offers only an introduction to his work. Salt Spring allowed Schubart to reinvent himself, and in the process, Salt Spring Island has been permanently changed. His houses, with their intuitive logic and design, reveal his character. He relentlessly pursued his designs, visiting sites, listening for sounds, imagining views from inside. That specificity informed his craft and resolved the challenge of each site. On this small island, it was not so much the sparsely populated community that supported Schubart's reach as it was the scope of his experience, talent, and personality. Over time, his architectural work became richer, deeper, and, in a restrained way, more elaborate. Reflecting on his career a few years before he died, Schubart described his success this way:

> I'd say that my fame on the island, if you could call it that, is mostly involved in very careful siting and site development, and concern for the landscape and the trees. In that sense, organic. Also, we have a very limited series of building materials available here—local cedar and glass. I'm not interested in showy stuff. It's organic in the sense that it's natural. Providing a very personal, careful and thoughtful service to people is organic in a community sense, and I don't do funky buildings. Some people define "organic" in different ways. But, I've tried to practice in a way which was really a contribution to the community and to not desecrate nature. Let's put it that way.[13]

Many consider his houses highly functional sculptures. They populate the island as tributes to his talent, unnoticed in groves of cedar trees until visitors arrive on their sites. Each house solves several problems: how to secure the best view with maximum privacy, how to capitalize on light in the rainy British Columbia weather, how to fit in among the trees and nature, how to use local materials. According to the artist Robert Bateman: "Hank's houses are like a Japanese pot. The Japanese make sure the inside works and let the outside just happen."[14] Most importantly, Schubart sought to satisfy his clients' needs. "I have two great concerns when it comes to designing a home," he said. "That it is carefully and beautifully related to the land and that each house represents the needs of the clients."[15] As his homes pass into the hands of new owners, their simple elegance endures.

LEFT: Pred house, interior courtyard with its abundant skylights and outrigger soffits.
ABOVE: Pred house, front view. Schubart's challenge was to site the house on a rocky hill.

ABOVE: Vidalin house, dining room. This is one of the largest and most elaborate houses Schubart designed on Salt Spring Island. The interior finish is refined, largely reflecting the owner's gourmet taste. Groomed terraces form the approach. The rising roof dips and turns, bringing in the light and creating intimate spaces. FACING: Vidalin house, outdoor barbecue on the back porch, as Schubart designed it. FACING INSET: Schubart's sketch of the barbecue.

Ro. SKETCH OF BBQ
& BAKE OVEN - ARRANGED
TO RESPECT WINDOW 1/2" = 1'-0"

LEFT: Southend house, pool and back deck. Schubart's design called for blasting into the surrounding rock to create a buildable site. He insisted that the interior courtyard be a livable area. ABOVE: Southend house, beams defining and expanding the living and dining rooms. Courtesy of Robert Barnard Design, Ltd.

AFTERWORD

HARMONIC PLEASURES

**FEW FORTUNATE ARCHITECTS** develop bonds with clients that carry them over the course of their careers, allowing them the opportunity to work together on multiple projects. My client relationship with Jane Hickie and Michele Dunkerley spans six projects over twenty-five years, involving the creation of new houses and the renovation of existing ones. I like to think that our mutual respect and admiration, as well as a love and recognition of special places, have allowed us to create together memorable homes.

Jane and Michele found Salt Spring Island and brought me to look at a house sited in a narrow finger channel. The arrival was mysterious: one enters the property along a ridge, and the path then weaves downward through several switchbacks until, at the last turn, the cedar roof appears just at eye level. The final approach was on foot, down into a carved-out front court, under the sweeping roof and into the core of the house.

This is one of my favorite setups for drama (I differ strongly from Witold Rybczynski, who much prefers to approach a house from below—lots of "underwear" to think about for the designer is my attitude). I loved the organic shape of the roof, its thickly crusted shakes and crisply detailed ridge of skylights. The roof was so fitted to the envelope of trees that it was almost alive itself—like the cap of a mushroom concealing the rest of the plant below.

As all Frank Lloyd Wright fans know, the right way to follow up a low, mysterious entry is to explode spatially—to balance the low shade with high light, the sense of intimacy and containment with lofty space and dramatic views. This house did that in spades, and I knew immediately that my clients had found their home.

The house had been described as a "Schubart," a name that I later found to be well known on the island. Although I was unfamiliar with his work, I could see that he knew what he was doing. My job was going to be one of editing—eliminating some of the eccentricities (like an indoor swimming pool), removing the dated elements, and returning the house to a state of harmonic pleasure.

A dialogue begins between the original and renovating architects as the house gets stripped to its elemental design. Why did he put the stairs here? If that door to the balcony is open, isn't it remarkable how the breeze picks up? It is an attempt to dissect the choreography of the dance, the experiences that the first architect embedded in his design that can be re-released for each user of the house.

Our first task was to find the right contractor with whom to collaborate, and we couldn't have been more fortunate in the choice of Gord Speed. He is not only a thoughtful, meticulous craftsman, but also an excellent contractor with prior experience on Schubart homes. His insights helped us with making appropriate choices as we moved through design and into construction.

The hub of the house is a great room divided by a stairwell to the lower level. It is crowned by a beautiful wooden ceiling topped with skylights. Spinning off this multisided room were two wings—a kitchen–utility room–carport and a bedroom wing complete with that indoor pool. The lower level contained more bedrooms, a boathouse, and unfinished space.

We preserved the character of the main room, updating the fireplace and reducing the scale of the banded skylights, which have become less necessary as the climate has warmed up. Knowing well my clients' penchant for informal dinner parties that start in the kitchen, it was truly a pleasure to update the galley layout with new cabinetry, finishes, and appliances. Joining the design cooks in the kitchen was Robin Black, an interior designer from San Antonio who has also worked with these clients since our first project in 1984. Robin's indefatigable spirit and classic modernist bent work well with Jane and Michele's tailored taste and high humor, making this long-distance collaboration zesty and inspired. It was Robin, for example, who was able to wrangle the exterior light fixtures from a famous fabricator in San Antonio—their punched-metal surfaces are a wonderful complement to the natural wood-and-glass exterior (see pages 8–10 and 103–105).

Further changes were made in the two bedroom areas: the main-level wing became a master retreat, and the lower level was outfitted with a suite of bedrooms, sittings areas, and much-needed storage. The master wing now includes a library and studio space where the owners can sequester themselves with reading, writing, and art projects. This retreat is made especially appealing because the uphill side of the rooms is partially subterranean, the windows providing a hedgehog view up into a Japanese maple and the front-court garden. Elsewhere in the same set of rooms, the views are far more expansive, down and out to the lagoon. Each vista is appealing, and the juxtaposition allows each to retain visual freshness.

On the lower level, Schubart arranged the bedrooms with their own outdoor terraces. These we barely touched, turning our attention to bathrooms, a "cave" for watching television, and a light-filled playroom. This floor has a lovely connection to the garden and the lagoon, without any of the usual sense of "second-class" accommodations often associated with lower-level bedrooms. The goal throughout was to remain in harmony with Schubart's design while reflecting our own vision of the home's contemporary purposes.

As I worked on the house, I was struck by how familiar it felt. Clearly, Schubart was influenced by Frank Lloyd Wright, but who else had shaped the shaper?

Jane and Michele became curious. They got the story of Schubart's move to Salt Spring from Northern California, and with that came the important nugget that he had worked with Bill Wurster at Wurster Bernardi & Emmons. When I was at Stanford in the early 1970s, Bill Wurster was one of my gods. His work was so understated, but fresh and humane. He was famous for his approaches—that whole sequence of small moves that manipulated light, space, sun, shade, air, shelter. And of course, he wrote the book on houses that fit into rugged northwestern settings. His houses were simple indigenous structures wholly at peace in their settings.

Having reached the midpoint of my own career, I strive for this same natural grace of form and deftness in the siting of my own work, and this is what I recognized in the Schubart house. I am confident that my exposure to Wurster and my time in California gave me an added appreciation for Schubart's architecture and allowed me to meld my contributions more seamlessly to his original work.

Further investigation for this book unearthed a second architectural connection—both Schubart and I had worked briefly for Jose Sert in our early apprenticeships (my tenure there was so brief that it no longer makes it onto my unabridged resume). From what I have now read of Schubart's time with Sert, I think I admire the architect more, which teaches me another thing about Schubart.

He was very opinionated about architecture. Did any Frank Lloyd Wright disciple escape that trait?

Maybe that is why Salt Spring turned out to be a fertile place for his blend of creativity, individualism, and respect for the land. These days it is becoming rare to find a place that has been defined by one architect. All of us are working on a more global stage. And yet, as I think this book illustrates, an intangible yet powerful link can be forged over decades of work among the same rocks and inlets and meandering roadways. Schubart never lost his inventiveness: each site, each client was both wholly new and also familiar. His works belong to the land and the people of that remarkable island.

HEATHER H. MCKINNEY, Founding Principal
McKinney York Architects, FAIA, LEED AP

ILLUSTRATIONS

NOTES

PREFACE

1. Henry A. Schubart, Jr., telephone interview by Indira Berndtson, March 23, 1995 (Frank Lloyd Wright Archives, Frank Lloyd Wright Foundation, Taliesin West, Scottsdale, Arizona; hereafter cited as Wright Archives).
2. Dicker, Susan, "Distinct Features Characterize Architect's Designs," *Gulf Islands Driftwood*, April 8, 1988.

CHAPTER 1: FIRST GLIMPSE

1. Henry A. Schubart, Jr., to Linda Schubart Hawkins, January 28, 1985 (Linda Hawkins's personal collection); also, Linda Hawkins, interview by the author and Jane Hickie, Berkeley, California, October 20, 2007. Schubart's maternal grandparents were Louis and Clara Werner.
2. Two years younger than his brother, Mark Schubart would become a dean at the Julliard School of Music and then a vice president at Lincoln Center and the founder and chairman emeritus of the Lincoln Center Institute for the Arts in Education.
3. Henry Schubart, interview by Berndtson. Wright's *An Autobiography* was first published in 1932.
4. Henning, *At Taliesin*, 1.
5. It is worth printing young Schubart's initial letter to Taliesin (preserved in the Wright Archives) in its entirety:

> Dear Mr. Wright
>
> I read with pleasure an article in the New York Times about your "Taliesin Fellowship," a beautiful venture and one which I would love to share.
>
> I was lucky enough to find my own personality during the two years that I spent in France. Much of my time was occupied with an intensive study of the French language, which I now speak fluently and more vital still my life work, painting!

At first I worked as a freelance in the South of France forming ideas and working them out very simply on canvas; then, finding myself lacking in the actual form and technique of painting, worked with a Belgian painter, Vietinghoff, in Paris, from whom I learnt the chemistry and inroads of the "métier." I also formed a close friendship with Martin Baer, who became my confidant and devoted co-worker. He, being a Chicagoan, you might know of him.

Now that I'm back in America and living on a farm I feel that working alone has been too great a problem to tackle and until I saw the article was very much at a loss as to what to do. I feel that my experiences are too limited for me to just paint and your plan appealed to me because of its combination of the creative, the craftsmanship and physical work, all of which I find lacking in the "Art" schools and regular schools.

As a younger boy I always enjoyed and still find an outlet in gardening, carpentry and being a general handyman and as all of these things are contained in your bookless school it seems like a dream come true.

Two months ago having read your autobiography very eagerly I found in you a man of my ideals and a sympathetic and understanding individual so that writing to you and asking whether I might be able to share this beautiful venture, thrills me. If you feel that I am worthwhile material for your fellowship I would like to know more about it.

Very Sincerely Yours,

Henry A. Schubart Jr.

6. Karl Jensen, secretary of the Taliesin Fellowship, to Henry A. Schubart, Jr., August 19, 1933 (Wright Archives).

7. Wright, *Letters to Apprentices*, 8.

8. Henry Schubart, interview by Berndtson.

CHAPTER TWO: WRIGHT'S TALIESIN

1. Henry Schubart, interview by Berndtson.

2. In December 1933, a new brochure described the program at Taliesin and listed the charter members of the Taliesin Fellowship, now called "Fellows." Henry Schubart of New York City was a charter fellow. Others there at the time included Edgar Tafel, John and MaryBud Lautner, Irvin "Bud" Shaw, Eugene Masselink, Alden and Vada Dow, Nicholas Ray, and Yen Liang.

3. Henry Schubart, interview by Berndtson.

4. Ibid. The Willey house was a project in Minneapolis, Minnesota. Built for Malcolm and Nancy Willey in 1934, the house was based on the second design that Wright created, the first being deemed too costly for the owner, a college administrator. In the end, the house was 1,200 square feet. For more information on this Wright project, see http://www.thewilleyhouse.com.

5. Several letters were exchanged about the piano matter; see Henry A. Schubart, Jr., to Frank Lloyd Wright, December 20, 1933; Wright to Henry Schubart, Sr., February 26, 1934; and Henry Schubart, Sr., to Wright, March 5, 1934 (all letters in the Wright Archives).

6. Henry Schubart, interview by Berndtson.

7. The "At Taliesin" columns were published from February 1934 through 1937. The first column that Schubart collaborated on was published March 8, 1934, and entitled "Whitman Sounds Note for Taliesin's Motive." It was published in the *Madison (WI) Times*. The second was published in the *Wisconsin State Journal* on June 4, 1934. For more information, see Henning, *At Taliesin*.

8. Pauline Schubart to Frank Lloyd Wright, March 15, 1934 (Wright Archives).

9. Pauline Schubart, "At Taliesin," *Capital Times* (Madison, Wisconsin), August 24, 1934, and "At Taliesin," *Wisconsin State Journal*, August 28, 1934. In these columns, Pauline hints at what motivated her son to join the Fellowship at Taliesin:

> I came to visit my son, an apprentice at Taliesin, expecting to find him at school. In other words experiencing some kind of institutional social life . . . [Taliesin] is composed of people who have felt a definite lack in their previous experience whether in the home, the school or the college in the homes they have felt "possessed." In the schools and colleges they have felt the inapplicability of what they were being taught and the remoteness of that life from the one they would be called upon to meet in the outside world. They have come to Taliesin in the hope that they will find a way there of living more fully and of making something significant of every day for themselves in no matter how small a way.

10. Henry Schubart, interview by Berndtson; see also Frank Lloyd Wright to Henry Schubart, Jr., May 6, 1935 (Wright Archives.)

11. Henry A. Schubart, Jr., to Frank Lloyd Wright, August 26, 1934 (Wright Archives).

12. Henry A. Schubart, Jr., to Frank Lloyd Wright and Olgivanna Wright, December 15, 1934 (Wright Archives).

13. Ibid.

14. Henry Schubart, interview by Berndtson.

15. Frank Lloyd Wright to Henry A. Schubart, Jr., May 6, 1935 (Wright Archives).

16. Henry Schubart, interview by Berndtson.

17. Broadacre City was a utopian idea conceived by Wright in his book *The Disappearing City* (1932). Residents of Broadacre City would own homesteads of at least one acre, participate in an agrarian economy, and live in decentralized but functional communities. However, like suburbanites, they would be dependent on automobile transportation, and city planners panned the idea. Despite this, Wright held fast to his utopian vision until his death.

18. Frank Lloyd Wright to Henry A. Schubart, Jr., December 4, 1935 (Wright Archives).

19. Henry Schubart, interview by Berndtson.

20. Hemp later remarried, and it was under the name Lilo Raymond that she became widely admired for her haunting black-and-white interiors and still-life photography. In the introduction to a book on her work, Raymond credits Schubart with buying her her first camera, a Graflex Speed Graphic (Raymond, *Revealing Light*, 1989).

21. Henry Schubart, interview by Berndtson.

22. Ibid.

CHAPTER 3: THE MAKING OF A WEST COAST MODERNIST

1. Lilo Raymond, interview by the author, April 12, 2007, Eddyville, New York.

2. Henry Schubart, interview by Berndtson.

3. Henry A. Schubart, Jr., to Frank Lloyd Wright, July 16, 1946 (Wright Archives).

4. William Wurster, the founding name partner of WB&E, was a recognized leader in the development of mid-twentieth-century residential architecture. In 1951, Wurster became the dean of architecture at the University of California, Berkeley.

5. Treib, *Everyday Modernism*, 58, 89.

6. Ibid., 89.

7. Henry Schubart, interview by Berndtson.

8. Ibid.

9. Phyllis Friedman, interview by the author and Jane Hickie, May 8, 2007, Hillsborough, California.

10. Henry A. Schubart, Jr., and Howard A. Friedman, "The Case for the Small Office."

11. *New York Times Magazine*, October 30, 1960 (unknown page; clipping in the Howard Friedman Collection, Environmental Design Archives, University of California, Berkeley). These low-cost designs so impressed a delegation of Russian housing experts in 1960 that they bought one of the plans, complete with wallpaper, kitchen linoleum, and all its furnishings.

12. The name of the new building was chosen to honor the first archbishop of San Francisco, the Dominican friar Joseph Sadoc Alemany. In 1850, he requested that the first religious community of women be established in California—now the Dominican Sisters of San Rafael.

13. *Dominican College Alumnae News*, "Archbishop Alemany Library." For more on the college plans for the library, see also, *Newsletter*, "Sister Patrick—College President," 3.

14. The AIA, the American Library Association, and the National Book Committee awarded this prize to Schubart and Friedman and the Archbishop Alemany Library (see the *Daily Pacific Builder* [Monrovia, Calif.], April 6, 1964). In 1966, Schubart was asked to design another structure at Dominican University, a sunken amphitheater that would also be home to the Marin County Summer Shakespeare Festival. To segregate the audience from the stage—and help amplify stage voices and block noise from a nearby freeway—he designed a moat at the stage front. Opened in 1967, the amphitheater, which seats 750 people on contoured benches with wooden backs, is now where the university's commencement ceremonies are held.

15. Gervaise Valpey, president emerita of the San Domenico School, interview by the author and Jane Hickie, San Rafael, California, March 30, 2007. Additional articles highlighting the new campus were in the *San Francisco Examiner*, December 10, 1965, and the *Independent-Journal* (Marin County), October 19, 1965.

16. *Time*, "Modern Living: Do It Yourself."

17. Dan Schubart, interview by the author and Jane Hickie, Nanaimo, British Columbia, May 28, 2008; Peter Schubart, interview by the author and Jane Hickie, Los Altos, California, May 13, 2007.

18. Anderson, "Success Story of a Delinquent Lot."

19. In a rare public role, Schubart accepted an honorary designation in 1965 as consulting architect for the Civic Center Plaza competition in San Francisco. Sponsored by the Art Commission of the City of San Francisco, this was an international competition to develop the plaza's central area. Schubart organized a distinguished board of jurists to select the winning entrant. Schubart was the professional adviser; Thomas Church, Sybil Moholy-Nagy, and Luis Barragan were among the jurists whom he selected. The contest was won by a young Bulgarian couple, Ivan Tzvetin and Angela Danadjieva. Danadjieva went on to become a highly regarded landscape designer. Their design called for layers of stone to mimic pages of the city's history. When the city refused to build the plaza design, for whatever reason, this decision disappointed Schubart, adding local unhappiness to his general dissatisfaction with U.S. politics.

20. Claude Stoller, interview by the author and Jane Hickie, Berkeley, California, May 17, 2008.

21. Britton, "The Neighborhoods Need Our Attention," 4, 5.

22. Obituary of Henry Schubart, *San Francisco Chronicle*, February 20, 1988.

CHAPTER 4: AN EMERGING SENSIBILITY

1. Ruth-Marion Baruch and Pirkle Jones met as students in a photography class at the California School of Fine Arts in San Francisco (now the San Francisco Art Institute). The couple became friends and collaborators with Edward Weston, Ansel Adams, Imogen Cunningham, and Dorothea Lange. As was said of Baer and Piaskowski, and might have been said of the Joneses and Schubarts, "the two had a great love and a lively circle of friends that spanned from the Bohemians to the Beats" (Julian Guthrie, "Nata Piaskowski—Photographer Known for Superb Composition," *San Francisco Chronicle*, August 28, 2004).

2. Henry A. Schubart, Jr., to Walter C. Kidney, associate editor, *Progressive Architecture*, November 11, 1968 (Schubart architectural files).

3. The "Declaration of Restrictions," adopted in 1963 and in effect until January 1, 2000, required each structure to be approved by the Architectural Committee, defined as either Jones and Baruch or the surviving member of the couple if one died. The original list of approved architects and architectural firms included Henry Schubart; Del Campo & Clark (Martin Del Campo was a former associate at Schubart and Friedman); Joseph Esherick; Aaron Green; and Wurster Bernardi & Emmons, among others. The

restrictions addressed the location of a residence on a parcel, the grading of lots, and the color of the exterior paint. Driveways were for transportation access only; utilities had to be buried; only domestic pets were allowed on the premises; no temporary buildings were to be erected; and restrictions on signs and garbage placement were carefully set out.

4. Schubart to Kidney, November 11, 1968.

5. Pirkle Jones and Ruth-Marion Baruch, "Description of the [Marin County] Subdivision Written to Market the Remaining Two Lots to the Public," n.d. (Pirkle Jones Foundation, Marin County, California).

6. The concrete flooring emits radiant heat for the house, and its tan color includes 300 pounds of mineral color in the cement. The owners liked the color of the concrete floors because it looked "dirty." Jones applied the nearly eight coats of wax to the floor himself.

7. Henry A. Schubart, Jr., to Mr. and Mrs. Tom Guldman, February 24, 1972 (Schubart architectural files).

8. Schubart to Kidney, November 11, 1968.

9. Kidney, "Open Pavilion on Virgin Land," 130–133.

10. Schubart to Kidney, November 11, 1968.

CHAPTER 5: SALT SPRING ISLAND

1. Kahn, *Salt Spring*, 277.

2. Dan Schubart interview.

3. A pan-abode is a structure in which logs are fitted together with tongue and groove, giving the appearance of log cabin but with a better fit.

4. Maggie Schubart, Paul Schubart, and Gabrielle Schubart, interview by the author and Jane Hickie, Salt Spring Island, July 16, 2006; Peter Schubart interview.

5. Henry A. Schubart, Jr., Examination for Discovery of Henry A. Schubart, Jr., December 7, 1993, 12; this was evidence in the lawsuit Edgar Fosburgh Kaiser, Jr. v. Bufton's Flowers Ltd., Kenneth Hubert Bufton, North Shore Plumbing & Heating Co. Ltd., Charles Coleman, Henry Roper, Marcia Coleman and Ronald Coleman, a partnership carrying on business under the name and style of "North Shore Electric (1972) Co.," Lauder Bros. & Tate Builders Ltd., Henry Schubart Jr., Michael Schubart, Brian McHugh, Peter Jones & Associates Ltd., Hou Kwong & Associates, K. R. Kishi Ltd. and S. I. Taylor & Associates Ltd., a partnership carrying on business under the name and style of "Jones Kwong Kishi," J. D. Kern & Company, Ltd., A&B Masonry

174 Ltd., Alliance Sheet Metal Works Ltd., City of Vancouver, ABC Company LTD., DEF Company LTD, John Doe I and Joe Doe II (hereafter cited as "Kaiser Lawsuit").

6. Created in 1966 as part of President Johnson's War on Poverty, the Model Cities Program was a federal urban-aid program that emphasized urban planning, the rehabilitation of urban areas, the delivery of social services, and citizen participation.

7. Henry A. Schubart, Jr., to Mr. and Mrs. Paul Beauchemin, August 10, 1968; October 20, 1968; and February 7, 1969 (Schubart architectural files).

8. Henry A. Schubart, Jr., to Alberto and family (no last name given), Sausalito, California, September 13, 1970 (Schubart architectural files).

9. Henry A. Schubart, Jr., Examination for Discovery of Henry A. Schubart, Jr., April 13, 1993, 28 (Kaiser Lawsuit).

10. Martin Ogilvie, interview by the author, Salt Spring Island, October 1, 2008.

11. Henry A. Schubart Jr., to Mr. and Mrs. Paul Beauchemin, December 18, 1968 (Schubart architectural files).

12. Norman Twa, interview by the author and Jane Hickie, Salt Spring Island, August 19, 2007.

13. Eddy Jang, interview by the author, Salt Spring Island, July 16, 2008.

14. Ray Hill, telephone interview by the author, February 27, 2008.

15. Schubart deposition, Dec. 7, 1993, 6 (Kaiser Lawsuit).

CHAPTER 6: THE PRACTICE FLOURISHES

1. Mark Proctor, interview by the author and Jane Hickie, Ladysmith, British Columbia, January 8, 2007.

2. Henry A. Schubart, Jr., to Mr. and Mrs. Paul Beauchemin, February 7, 1969.

3. Located on fifty-four acres on Cotton Bay, the house on Eleuthera had its own soundproof powerhouse with generator plants and a complete desalination plant that could produce nearly six hundred gallons of fresh water an hour from seawater. Finished in 1972, by 1975 the house was for sale (for $2.75 million; overall cost figures were probably closer to $4 million). Roberson Ward Associates, Ltd., Nassau, and Henry Schubart, Jr., Ganges, British Columbia, were credited as architects of the house.

4. Schubart deposition, April 13, 1993, 59 (Kaiser Lawsuit).

5. Becky Kaiser, interview by the author and Jane Hickie, Eugene, Oregon, November 11, 2007.

6. Tom Toynbee, telephone interview by the author, January 15, 2008.

7. Kahn, *Salt Spring*, 287–289.

8. Henry A. Schubart, Jr., to Amy McCleod, secretary-treasurer of School District #64, Salt Spring Island, December 13, 1982 (Schubart architectural files).

9. Henry A. Schubart, Jr., to Mr. and Mrs. Drobac, April 29, 1968 (Schubart architectural files). On February 17, 1969, Martin Drobac wrote to Hank expressing some concern: "Dear Hank, Ha Ha Ha Ha Ha Ha Ha Ha Ha Ha Ha Ha Ha (sob). I had always thought myself a reasonable man, unreasonably so, it seems. I started out thinking in terms of $20 a foot. When you suggested it might be $25, I flicked a manicured hand, in the manner of a man who either has great wealth, or has never learned the price of a roof and a hot square. That seemed exorbitant, but what the hell. But $50! Regards, Martin" (Schubart architectural files).

10. Henry A. Schubart, Jr., to Mr. and Mrs. Martin Drobac, November 23, 1969 (Schubart architectural files).

11. Ilse Leader, interview by the author and Tania Kingsbury, Salt Spring Island, October 1, 2007.

12. Christopher Secor, interview by the author and Jane Hickie, Mill Valley, California, March 30, 2007.

CHAPTER 7: VILLAGE ARCHITECT

1. Sonja and Ted Baker, interview by the author and Jane Hickie, Salt Spring Island, August 29, 2007.

2. Margaret and Basil Franey, interview by the author and Jane Hickie, Salt Spring Island, August 12, 2007.

3. Margaret and Blair Dymond, interview by the author and Jane Hickie, Salt Spring Island, August 26, 2006.

4. Jeremy and Jane Winter, interview by the author and Jane Hickie, Salt Spring Island, October 9, 2006.

5. Proctor interview.

6. The information about Schubart's working methods came from the following sources: Robert Barnard, interview by the author and Jane Hickie, Salt Spring Island, June 8, 2006, and July 4, 2006; Paul Schubart, interview by the author and Jane Hickie, Salt Spring Island, January 4, 2008; Michael Schubart, interview by the author and Jane Hickie, Salt Spring Island, July 15, 2007, and September 4, 2007; Matthew Schubart, interview by the author and Jane Hickie, Mercer Island, Washington, November 5, 2006; Mario Szijarto,

176   interview by the author and Jane Hickie, Sidney, British Columbia, September 7, 2008; Gordon Speed, interview by the author and Jane Hickie, Salt Spring Island, August 30, 2006; and, Twa interview.

7. Richard Dakin, interview by the author and Jane Hickie, Salt Spring Island, June 6, 2007.

8. Barnard interview.

9. Speed interview.

10. Barnard interview.

11. Speed interview.

12. John and Claire Pickering, interview by the author and Jane Hickie, Salt Spring Island, September 4, 2006.

13. Uli Temmel, interview by the author, Salt Spring Island, August 26, 2008. This was a comment a third party reported to Temmel that Schubart had made.

14. Dakin interview.

15. Speed interview.

16. Henry Schubart, interview by Berndtson. Schubart offered a continuing-education class on "building your own space" in the late 1970s. In this class, students brought their projects (such as deck plans) to class, which was held at his big Schubart house on Old Scott Road.

17. Maggie Schubart, interview by the author and Jane Hickie, Salt Spring Island, April 7, 2007.

18. Paul Schubart interview; Matthew Schubart interview.

19. Maggie Schubart, interview by the author and Jane Hickie, Salt Spring Island, July 16, 2006.

20. Robert Bateman, interview by the author and Jane Hickie, Salt Spring Island, August 16, 2007.

21. A fourth development, Musgrave Landing, did not involve Schubart. He was, however, involved in the Unger property development on Beaver Point Road. But the most well-known developments on Salt Spring Island remain Reginald Hill, Maracaibo Estates, and Channel Ridge (see Kahn, *Story of an Island*, 290–291).

22. For more on Maracaibo, see Bazzard and Bazzard, *Magic of Maracaibo*.

23. Gabrielle Schubart, telephone interview by the author, January 21, 2009.

24. Rae and Ian Jessiman, interview by the author and Jane Hickie, Salt Spring Island, September 2, 2006.

1. Susan Dicker, "Distinct Features Characterize Architect's Designs," *Gulf Islands Driftwood*, April 6, 1988.

2. Behind Schubart's initial construction was an active secondary market in gutter installation, and many clients added gutters after Schubart was finished with their houses.

3. Temmel interview.

4. Charlotte and Nick Acuros, interview by the author and Jane Hickie, Salt Spring Island, September 2, 2007; Linda and Michael Overholt, interview by the author and Jane Hickie, Salt Spring Island, August 27, 2006.

5. Pickering interview.

6. Michael Schubart interview.

7. Twa interview.

8. Patrick Normal, interview by the author, Salt Spring Island, July 26, 2007.

9. Mallory Pred, interview by the author and Jane Hickie, Salt Spring Island, July 14, 2006.

10. Gerald Godfrey, telephone interview by the author and Jane Hickie, September 19, 2008.

11. Audrey and Bryan Williams, interview by the author and Jane Hickie, Salt Spring Island, October 8, 2006.

12. Linda Overholt interview.

13. Schubart, interview by Berndtson.

14. Bateman interview.

15. Quoted in Dicker, "Distinct Features Characterize Architect's Designs."

BIBLIOGRAPHY

Acuros, Charlotte, and Nick Acuros. Interview by the author and Jane Hickie, Salt Spring Island, September 2, 2007.

Anderson, Curtiss M. "Success Story of a Delinquent Lot." Unknown publication, n.d. In "Project Clippings Scrapbook," Howard Friedman Collection, Environmental Design Archives, University of California, Berkeley.

Baker, Sonja, and Ted Baker. Interview by the author and Jane Hickie, Salt Spring Island, August 29, 2007.

Barnard, Robert. Interview by the author and Jane Hickie, Salt Spring Island, June 8 and July 4, 2006.

Bateman, Robert. Interview by the author and Jane Hickie, Salt Spring Island, August 16, 2007.

Bazzard, Sally, and Charles Bazzard. *The Magic of Maracaibo: Stories of the Athol Peninsula*. Salt Spring Island, B.C.: Barnyard Graphics, 1998.

Britton, James. "The Neighborhoods Need Our Attention: Can Community Design Centers Do Any Good? How?" *Vital Questions*, n.d. American Institute of Architects.

Dakin, Richard. Interview by the author and Jane Hickie, Salt Spring Island, June 6, 2007.

Dominican College Alumnae News. "Archbishop Alemany Library." Spring 1963. San Rafael, Calif.

Dymond, Margaret, and Blair Dymond. Interview by the author and Jane Hickie, Salt Spring Island, August 26, 2006.

Franey, Margaret, and Basil Franey. Interview by the author and Jane Hickie, Salt Spring Island, August 12, 2007.

Friedman, Phyllis. Interview by the author and Jane Hickie, Hillsborough, California, May 8, 2007.

Godfrey, Gerald. Telephone interview by the author and Jane Hickie, September 19, 2008.

Hawkins, Linda. Interview by the author and Jane Hickie, Berkeley, California, October 20, 2007.

Henning, Randolph C. *At Taliesin: Newspaper Columns by Frank Lloyd Wright and the Taliesin Friendship, 1934–1937*. Carbondale: Southern Illinois Univ. Press, 1992.

Hill, Ray. Telephone interview by the author, February 27, 2008.

Jang, Eddy. Interview by the author, Salt Spring Island, July 16, 2008.

Jessiman, Rae, and Ian Jessiman. Interview by the author and Jane Hickie, Salt Spring Island, September 2, 2006.

Kahn, Charles. *Salt Spring: The Story of an Island*. Madeira Park, B.C.: Harbour, 1998.

Kaiser, Becky. Interview by the author and Jane Hickie, Eugene, Oregon, November 11, 2007.

Kidney, Walter C. "Open Pavilion on Virgin Land." *Progressive Architecture*, March 1969, 130–133.

Leader, Ilse. Interview by the author and Tania Kingsbury, Salt Spring Island, October 1, 2007.

Newsletter [of Dominican College (now University), San Rafael, Calif.]. "Sister Patrick—College President." Vol. 3, no. 1 (February 1961).

New York Times Magazine. October 30, 1960.

Normal, Patrick. Interview by the author, Salt Spring Island, July 26, 2007.

Ogilvie, Martin. Interview by the author, Salt Spring Island, October 1, 2008.

Overholt, Linda, and Michael Overholt. Interview by the author and Jane Hickie, Salt Spring Island, August 27, 2006.

Pickering, Claire and John. Interview by the author and Jane Hickie, Salt Spring Island, September 4, 2006.

Pred, Mallory, and Ralph Pred. Interview by the author and Jane Hickie, Salt Spring Island, July 14, 2006.

Proctor, Mark. Interview by the author and Jane Hickie, Ladysmith, B.C., January 8, 2007.

Raymond, Lilo (Hemp). Interview by the author, Eddyville, New York, April 12, 2007.

———. *Revealing Light: Photographs*. Boston: Bullfinch, 1989.

Schubart, Dan. Interview by the author and Jane Hickie, Nanaimo, British Columbia, May 28, 2008.

Schubart, Gabrielle. Telephone interview by the author, January 21, 2009.

Schubart, Henry A., Jr. Examination for Discovery of Henry A. Schubart, Jr. April 13, 1993; October 8, 1993; and December 7, 1993 (Kaiser Lawsuit).

———. Telephone interview by Indira Berndtson, March 23, 1995. Frank Lloyd

Wright Archives. Courtesy of the Frank Lloyd Wright Foundation, Taliesin West, Scottsdale, Ariz.

Schubart, Henry A., Jr., and Howard A. Friedman. "The Case for the Small Office." Unknown publication, n.d. In "Project Clippings Scrapbook," Howard Friedman Collection, Environmental Design Archives, University of California, Berkeley.

Schubart, Maggie. Interview by the author and Jane Hickie, Salt Spring Island, June 7, 2006; April 7, 2007; August 5, 2007; and January 1, 2008.

Schubart, Maggie, Paul Schubart, and Gabrielle Schubart. Interview by the author and Jane Hickie, Salt Spring Island, July 16, 2006.

Schubart, Matthew. Interview by the author and Jane Hickie, Mercer Island, Washington, November 5, 2006.

Schubart, Michael. Interview by the author and Jane Hickie, Salt Spring Island, July 15, 2007, and September 4, 2007.

Schubart, Paul. Interview by the author and Jane Hickie, Salt Spring Island, January 1, 2008, and January 4, 2008.

Schubart, Peter. Interview by the author and Jane Hickie, Los Altos, California, May 13, 2007, and August 5, 2007.

Secor, Christopher. Interview by the author and Jane Hickie, Mill Valley, California, March 30, 2007.

Speed, Gordon. Interview by the author and Jane Hickie, Salt Spring Island, August 30, 2006.

Stoller, Claude. Interview by the author and Jane Hickie. Berkeley, Calif., May 17, 2008.

Szijarto, Mario. Interview by the author and Jane Hickie, Sidney, British Columbia, September 7, 2008.

Temmel, Uli. Interview by the author, Salt Spring Island, August 26, 2008.

Time. "Modern Living: Do It Yourself." June 30, 1952. http://www.time.com/time/magazine/article/0,9171,816577-1,00.html.

Toynbee, Tom. Telephone interview by the author, January 15, 2008.

Treib, Marc. *An Everyday Modernism: The Houses of William Wurster.* Berkeley and Los Angeles: Univ. of California Press, 1995.

Twa, Norman. Interview by the author and Jane Hickie, Salt Spring Island, August 19, 2007.

Valpey, Gervaise, president emerita, San Domenico School. Interview by the author and Jane Hickie, San Rafael, Calif., March 30, 2007.

Williams, Audrey, and Bryan Williams. Interview by the author and Jane Hickie, Salt Spring Island, October 8, 2006.

182   Winter, Jane, and Jeremy Winter. Interview by the author and Jane Hickie, Salt
        Spring Island, October 9, 2006.

Wright, Frank Lloyd. *An Autobiography*. Petaluma, Calif.: Pomegranate Commu-
        nications, 2005. First published in 1932 by Longmans, Green.

———. *Letters to Apprentices*. Edited by Bruce Brooks Pfeiffer. Fresno: Press at
        California State Univ., Fresno, 1982.